The Phantom of the Opera

The Original Gothic Mystery Romance –
Love, Obsession, and Terror

A Modern Translation

Adapted for the Contemporary Reader

Gaston Leroux

Translated by Tim Zengerink

Table of Contents

Preface - Message to the Reader 1

Introduction 4

Prologue 9

Chapter I Is it the Ghost? 13

Chapter II The New Margarita 24

Chapter III The Mysterious Reason 35

Chapter IV Box Five 43

Chapter V The Enchanted Violin 57

Chapter VI A Visit to Box Five 74

Chapter VII Faust and What Followed 77

Chapter VIII The Mysterious Brougham 93

Chapter IX At the Masked Ball 102

Chapter X Forget the Name of the Man's Voice 111

Chapter XI Above the Trap-Doors 117

Chapter XII Apollo's Lyre 125

Chapter XIII A Master-Stroke of the Trap-Door Lover 144

Chapter XIV The Singular Attitude of a Safety-Pin 156

Chapter XV Christine! Christine! 163

Chapter XVI Mme. Giry's Astounding Revelations as to Her
Personal Relations with the Opera Ghost 167

Chapter XVII The Safety-Pin Again 179

Chapter XVIII The Commissary, The Viscount and the Persian ... 186

Chapter XIX The Viscount and the Persian....................................... 192

Chapter XX In the Cellars of the Opera 200

Chapter XXI Interesting and Instructive Vicissitudes of a Persian
    in the Cellars of the Opera.. 215

Chapter XXII In the Torture Chamber 227

Chapter XXIII The Tortures Begin 235

Chapter XXIV "Barrels! ... Barrels! ... Any Barrels to Sell?"............. 242

Chapter XXV The Scorpion or the Grasshopper: Which? 252

Chapter XXVI The End of the Ghost's Love Story 260

Epilogue 270

Thank You for Reading 277

Preface - Message to the Reader

What If You Could Help Rebuild the Greatest Library in Human History?

Thousands of years ago, the Library of Alexandria stood as the crown jewel of human achievement — a sanctuary where the collected wisdom of every known civilization was gathered, preserved, and shared freely.

And then, it was lost.

Through fire, conquest, and the slow erosion of time, humanity lost not just books — but ideas, dreams, discoveries, and stories that could have changed the world forever.

Today, the Library of Alexandria lives again — and you are invited to be a part of its restoration.

Our mission is simple yet profound:

To rebuild the greatest library the world has ever known, and to translate all timeless works into every language and dialect, so that no seeker of knowledge is ever left behind again.

By joining our movement to rebuild the modern Library of Alexandria, you become part of an unprecedented mission:

- **Unlimited Access to the Greatest Audiobooks & eBooks Ever Written:**

  Instantly explore thousands of legendary works—Plato, Shakespeare, Jane Austen, Leo Tolstoy, and countless more. All instantly available to read or listen, placing a complete literary universe at your fingertips.

- **Beautiful Paperback & Deluxe Editions at Printing Cost**

  Own any title as an elegant paperback, deluxe hardcover, or stunning collectible boxset—offered to you at true printing cost, delivered straight to your door. Build your personal Library of Alexandria, crafted for beauty, built for durability, and worthy of proud display.

- **Fresh Translations for Modern Readers—in Every Language & Dialect**

  Enjoy timeless masterpieces reimagined in clear, contemporary language—no more outdated phrases or obscure references. Alongside the original versions, we're tirelessly translating these classics into every language and dialect imaginable, ensuring accessibility and understanding across cultures and generations.

- **Join a Global Renaissance of Literature & Knowledge**

  You directly support expanding our library, publishing deluxe editions at true cost, translating works into all global languages, and bringing humanity's greatest stories to people everywhere. By joining today, you're not just preserving a legacy of masterpieces; you set in motion a powerful wave of literary accessibility.

Become a Torchbearer of Knowledge.

Join us for free now at **LibraryofAlexandria.com**

Together, we will ensure that the light of human wisdom never fades again.

With gratitude and a shared love of knowledge,

The Modern Library of Alexandria Team

Visit:

www.libraryofalexandria.com

Or scan the code below:

Introduction

Behind the Mask: Mystery, Music, and Madness in the Paris Opera House

Few stories have captured the world's imagination like The Phantom of the Opera. Originally published in 1910 by French journalist and novelist Gaston Leroux, this haunting tale of passion, beauty, terror, and obsession has transcended its genre to become a lasting cultural phenomenon. Though most readers today know the story through its adaptations—most notably Andrew Lloyd Webber's record-breaking musical—the original novel is far more than a romantic melodrama. It is a suspenseful Gothic thriller, a historical mystery, and a psychologically rich meditation on the boundaries between genius and madness, love and control, humanity and monstrosity.

Set in the richly imagined and historically grounded Palais Garnier, the novel blends real architecture, urban legend, and supernatural suggestion into a compelling mystery. The Paris Opera House, with its shadowy underground lakes, secret passageways, and soaring chandeliers, becomes a character in its own right—an immense and opulent stage upon which human frailty and terror play out. Leroux's meticulous attention to detail, drawn from his background as a courtroom reporter and crime journalist, lends the story a gripping realism. Yet, this reality is always infused with myth and illusion, mirroring the story's central theme: that what lies behind the mask—both literal and symbolic—is often more frightening than the mask itself.

The Phantom of the Opera is not merely a ghost story; it is a tragedy rooted in psychological trauma, emotional isolation, and the destructive power of unrequited love. Through the character of Erik— the so-called Phantom—Leroux creates one of literature's most complex antiheroes: a brilliant composer, architect, and magician whose hideous face has condemned him to a life beneath the surface, both literally and emotionally. His obsession with the young soprano Christine Daaé unfolds with both tenderness and horror, blurring the line between protector and predator, love and manipulation. Leroux's tale asks us to consider: can genius exist without madness? Can love survive without freedom? And what is the cost of turning a man into a monster?

This introduction offers a deep exploration of the novel's themes, characters, historical background, and literary significance—inviting the modern reader to experience Leroux's masterpiece not only as a work of entertainment but as a timeless and richly layered story that continues to resonate with contemporary audiences.

Gaston Leroux and the Origins of the Phantom

To fully appreciate The Phantom of the Opera, one must first understand its creator. Gaston Leroux was born in Paris in 1868 and originally trained as a lawyer, but his passion for storytelling and investigation led him to journalism. He became a renowned crime reporter and theater critic, covering high-profile cases and courtrooms throughout France. His eye for detail, love of the theatrical, and fascination with mystery deeply informed his fiction. Before writing The Phantom of the Opera, he had already gained fame for his detective novel The Mystery of the Yellow Room (1907), one of the earliest locked-room mysteries.

By the time Leroux turned to the idea of a ghost haunting the Paris Opera House, he was already a master at blending real-world investigation with fictional intrigue. Indeed, part of the brilliance of The Phantom of the Opera is how seamlessly it weaves fiction with fact. The Palais Garnier, built between 1861 and 1875, was—and remains—one of the most iconic buildings in Paris. With its grand staircase, glittering chandeliers, hidden chambers, and even an underground lake, it was the perfect setting for a tale of hidden identities and shadowy secrets. Leroux took inspiration from actual rumors of a ghost in the opera house and reports of a chandelier accident that killed an audience member, using these as seeds to grow a much darker and more emotionally complex story.

Though the Phantom's origin is fictionalized, Leroux's approach resembles that of a true-crime writer uncovering a forgotten case. The novel opens as a semi-factual investigation: the narrator promises to reveal the real truth behind the mysterious "Opera Ghost" who terrorized the Parisian elite. This framing device gives the novel a journalistic tone, lending credibility to the most unbelievable events and encouraging readers to suspend disbelief. Leroux's real genius lies in how he gradually shifts the reader's attention from the external mystery—who is the Phantom?—to the internal torment of the Phantom himself.

Erik, the Phantom, is not a conventional villain. He is neither wholly monstrous nor wholly sympathetic. Rather, he is the embodiment of contradiction: an artist and a murderer, a genius and a recluse, a lover and a manipulator. His deformity, though never described in great detail, has made him an outcast since childhood. He has been caged, mocked, and rejected by every human community he has encountered. As a result, he has retreated into a world of illusions and music, believing that beauty and control are his only paths to acceptance. In Christine, he sees both a muse and a savior—but his love is poisoned by desperation, and his genius is scarred by loneliness.

This duality is what makes the novel so haunting. Leroux forces the reader to reckon with a central question: who is truly monstrous—the man with the disfigured face, or the society that could not see past it?

Masks, Music, and the Meaning of Love

One of the most compelling aspects of The Phantom of the Opera is its exploration of identity, performance, and the masks we wear—literally and figuratively. The Phantom hides his face behind a mask to shield the world from his deformity, but Christine too wears a kind of mask: that of obedience, innocence, and pliability. Raoul, her childhood friend and suitor, represents the traditional ideal of love and protection, but even he fails to understand Christine's inner world, her pull toward the Phantom, and the complexity of her emotional awakening.

Christine's journey lies at the heart of the novel. She is not a passive damsel in distress, but a woman torn between fear, fascination, and compassion. Her relationship with Erik is fraught, layered, and intensely human. Though she is horrified by his actions, she also recognizes his pain, his brilliance, and his desire for love. She sees what others cannot: that Erik's violence stems not from innate evil, but from years of rejection, humiliation, and heartbreak. This insight is what allows her, ultimately, to offer him the one thing he has never known—kindness.

The final scenes of the novel are some of the most poignant in all of Gothic literature. When Christine agrees to kiss the Phantom, not out of romantic love but from a place of deep empathy, she breaks through his shell of hatred and obsession. That single act of compassion redeems him, if only briefly. It is a moment of extraordinary emotional power: a man who has lived his whole life as a monster is, for a brief time, treated like a human being. In letting Christine go, Erik performs the first truly selfless act of his life. His death, lonely but peaceful, is a tragic end to a life misshaped by cruelty and misunderstanding.

Leroux's novel is filled with such emotional paradoxes. Love is shown not as a simple romantic ideal, but as a complex, often painful force. The Phantom loves Christine, but his love suffocates her. Raoul loves Christine, but he cannot understand her. Christine herself is caught between two worlds: one of light and order, the other of darkness and freedom. Her voice—her literal singing voice—becomes a symbol of her identity. She must learn to claim it, not as a puppet of the Phantom, nor as a possession of Raoul, but as her own.

In this way, The Phantom of the Opera transcends its surface story of mystery and horror. It becomes a deeply human tale of longing, isolation, redemption, and the possibility of forgiveness. Its themes resonate with anyone who has felt unseen, unloved, or trapped behind a mask. That is why the story continues to captivate audiences more than a century after its publication.

For the modern reader, this translation offers the chance to rediscover the raw, emotional power of Gaston Leroux's original vision. It strips away the layers of adaptation and musicality to reveal the beating heart of the story: a lonely genius, a compassionate woman, and a world too afraid to see beyond appearances. It is a story of music and madness, but above all, it is a story of the human soul—its deepest wounds, and its capacity for grace.

Prologue

The Opera ghost was real. He wasn't just made up by artists, superstitious managers, or the excited minds of ballet dancers, their mothers, or theater staff. No—he was a living person, even though he looked and acted like a ghost.

When I started digging through old records at the National Academy of Music, I quickly noticed strange connections between the ghost stories and one of the most shocking tragedies ever to shake the wealthy people of Paris. Soon, I began to think that this mystery could actually explain what had happened. These events weren't ancient— they happened only about thirty years ago. Even today, you could find older men who used to work at the Opera, trustworthy people, who remember it all clearly: the strange and dramatic disappearance of Christine Daaé, the vanishing of the Vicomte de Chagny, and the death of his older brother, Count Philippe, whose body was found by the lake in the basement of the Opera. But none of them had ever seriously thought that the ghost had anything to do with it.

At first, the truth was hard for me to believe. Every clue I found just made things more confusing and strange, almost like something beyond human understanding. More than once, I almost gave up, thinking I was chasing an illusion. But eventually, I found solid proof that confirmed what I had suspected all along—the Opera ghost was real.

That day, I had spent hours reading The Memoirs of a Manager, a light-hearted book by Moncharmin, one of the old Opera managers. He never believed in the ghost and joked about it constantly, even when he himself became a victim of the ghost's strange tricks involving mysterious envelopes of money.

Feeling frustrated, I left the library and happened to meet the current acting manager of the Opera. He was talking with a lively, well-dressed older man and introduced us. He already knew about my research and how I had been trying to track down the judge who handled the Chagny case, M. Faure. Nobody had seen him in years. It turns out he had been in Canada for fifteen years, and the first thing he did when he returned to Paris was visit the Opera for a free ticket. That man was Faure himself.

We spent the evening talking, and he told me everything he remembered about the Chagny case. Since there wasn't much hard evidence, he had assumed that the viscount had gone mad and his brother's death was an accident. Still, he believed something terrible had happened between the two brothers over Christine Daaé. He didn't know what happened to Christine or the viscount. When I brought up the ghost, he laughed. He had heard stories about strange things happening at the Opera and knew about the envelope incident. But he never found anything serious enough to act on as a judge. He did once talk to someone who claimed to see the ghost often. That person was the man everyone in Paris called "the Persian," someone known by all the Opera regulars. But the judge thought he was just imagining things.

I was fascinated by the Persian's story and wanted to find him before it was too late. Luckily, I tracked him down at his small apartment on Rue de Rivoli, where he had lived ever since—and where he passed away five months after my visit. At first, I wasn't sure if I could trust him. But after he spoke to me with complete honesty, shared everything he knew about the ghost, and gave me letters between Christine and the ghost, I had no more doubts. The Opera ghost wasn't just a story.

Some people have told me that those letters might have been faked by someone with a big imagination. But I was lucky to find other samples of Christine's handwriting and compared them. They matched perfectly. I also looked into the Persian's past and found that he was an honest man, not the kind to make up stories just for attention.

Many of the people who were seriously involved in the Chagny case—and who knew the Chagny family—agreed with me after I showed them all my notes and explained what I had found. One of them, General D——, even sent me a letter that I'd like to share here:

"Sir,

I strongly encourage you to publish your findings. I remember clearly that just before the disappearance of Christine Daaé, the famous singer, and the tragic event that shocked all of Faubourg Saint-Germain, people in the ballet lounge were often talking about the 'ghost.' The talk only stopped because of the tragedy that followed. But if the ghost can explain what happened—as I believe it can after hearing your explanation—then please, tell the story.

As strange as the ghost may seem, it makes more sense than the cruel idea that two brothers, who deeply loved each other, could end up in a deadly fight.

Sincerely, etc."

After gathering all my research, I went back through the Opera building—the place the ghost had once ruled. Everything I saw, everything I realized while walking through it, supported what the Persian had told me. And finally, I made an incredible discovery that confirmed everything. Years later, when workers were digging under the Opera to bury audio recordings of a singer's voice, they uncovered a body. I was able to prove right away that it was the ghost's. I even had the acting manager check it for himself. So, I don't care if some newspapers say it was someone who died during the time of the Commune—that's not true.

The people killed during the Commune weren't buried on that side of the Opera. I can even say exactly where their bones are, not far from the giant underground room that was once filled with supplies during the siege. I only found the ghost's body because of an unbelievable stroke of luck.

But we'll come back to the body and what should be done with it later. For now, I want to end this introduction by thanking everyone who helped me. That includes M. Mifroid, the police officer in charge when Christine first vanished; M. Remy and M. Mercier, both former managers; M. Gabriel, who led the chorus; and especially Mme. la Baronne de Castelot-Barbezac. She was once the "little Meg" from the story and is still proud of it. She was one of the most talented dancers and the daughter of Madame Giry, who managed the ghost's private box.

These people helped me more than I can say. Because of them, I'll be able to retell those moments of deep love and fear in great detail. I also want to thank the current Opera management for supporting my work, especially M. Messager, M. Gabion the acting manager, and the kind architect in charge of the building. He let me borrow the books of Charles Garnier, even though he wasn't sure I'd return them.

Lastly, I want to publicly thank my friend and former collaborator, M. J. Le Croze, for letting me use his amazing collection of theater books—even the rare ones he deeply valued.

GASTON LEROUX.

Chapter I
Is it the Ghost?

It was the night of a big celebration at the Opera. The managers, Messrs. Debienne and Poligny, were hosting one last show before they officially retired. In the middle of the excitement, a group of ballet girls burst into the dressing room of La Sorelli, one of the lead dancers. They had just come off stage after performing in Polyeucte. The room filled with noise and chaos—some girls were laughing nervously, others looked terrified.

Sorelli, who had wanted a quiet moment to practice the speech she was going to give the managers, turned toward the group, clearly annoyed. That's when little Jammes—a young dancer with bright blue eyes, rosy cheeks, and a cute turned-up nose—spoke up in a shaky voice:

"It's the ghost!"

She immediately locked the door.

Sorelli's dressing room was nicely decorated, with fancy but standard furniture: a big mirror, a couch, a dressing table, and a few cabinets. There were old portraits on the walls—famous performers from the past, reminding everyone of the Opera's long history. To the young ballet girls, who were used to sharing small, noisy dressing rooms full of shouting, singing, and teasing, Sorelli's room felt like a royal suite.

Though Sorelli tried to hide it, she was quite superstitious. Hearing the word "ghost" gave her a chill. She called Jammes a silly girl, but deep down, she took it seriously. She was one of the first people at the Opera to believe in the ghost.

"Did you really see him?" she asked.

"As clearly as I see you right now," Jammes replied, her legs shaking as she sank into a chair.

Then little Giry—dark-haired, dark-eyed, thin, and pale—added,

"If that was the ghost, he's really ugly!"

"Oh yes!" the rest of the girls agreed loudly.

Everyone started talking at once. They said the ghost had appeared dressed in a black tuxedo, suddenly standing right in front of them in the hallway. No one had seen where he came from. It was like he walked straight through the wall.

"Come on," said one girl, trying to stay calm. "You all see that ghost everywhere!"

And it was true. People at the Opera had been whispering about this mysterious figure for months—a man in a black suit who wandered through the halls like a shadow. He never spoke, and no one dared talk to him. He would appear out of nowhere and disappear just as quickly, without making a sound. At first, people laughed about the idea of a ghost dressed like a rich man or even a funeral director. But over time, the story grew, especially among the ballet girls. Some claimed they saw him often. Even those who joked about it were secretly nervous.

Whenever something strange or annoying happened—a trip, a prank, or even a missing makeup item—the ghost got blamed. If anything went wrong backstage, it was the Opera ghost's fault.

But had anyone really seen him? After all, there were plenty of men in black suits at the Opera. Still, the girls insisted this one was different. His suit looked like it was hanging on a skeleton. They said his face was a skull.

That part of the story came from Joseph Buquet, the head stagehand. He was one of the few people who had truly seen the ghost. He said he ran into him on a small staircase near the footlights that led down to the basement. The ghost only stayed for a second before vanishing. To anyone willing to listen, Joseph described him in detail:

"He's extremely thin, like his clothes are just hanging on bones. His eyes are deep and empty—just two black holes, like in a skull. His skin is tight over his bones and has a sickly yellow color. His nose is so small you can barely see it from the side, which makes his face hard to look at. He only has a few long strands of dark hair on his forehead and behind his ears."

Joseph wasn't known for telling stories. He was a serious, reliable man. People listened to him carefully. Not long after, others began saying they'd seen the same ghostly man with the skull face. At first, some thought it was just a prank played on Joseph by one of the crew. But soon, more strange things started happening—so strange that even the smartest people around started getting nervous.

One example stood out: A fireman—someone known for bravery—had gone into the basement to inspect things. He apparently went deeper than usual. Suddenly, he ran back to the stage, pale and shaking, nearly fainting into the arms of little Jammes's proud mother. What had scared him so badly? He claimed he had seen a floating head—on fire—coming right at him, with no body attached. And this was no ordinary man. This was Pampin, a tough fireman who wasn't afraid of anything, especially not fire.

The ballet girls were scared out of their minds. At first, the fiery head the fireman had seen didn't sound anything like the ghost Joseph Buquet described. But it didn't take long for the girls to convince themselves the ghost could change his head whenever he wanted. That made everything feel even more dangerous. If a tough fireman could panic and pass out, then it made sense for the girls—whether they danced in the front or back rows—to be nervous too. They started hurrying through dark hallways and avoiding dim corners completely.

The next day, Sorelli placed a horseshoe on the table near the stage-door guard's booth. From that point on, everyone who entered the Opera—except for audience members—had to touch the horseshoe before going upstairs. This wasn't just a made-up superstition. That horseshoe really existed, and if you go through the Cour de l'Administration entrance, you can still see it there today.

Back to that same night.

"It's the ghost!" little Jammes had shouted.

The room fell into complete silence. The only sound was the heavy breathing of the dancers. Jammes backed into the farthest corner of the room, clearly terrified.

"Listen," she whispered.

Everyone held their breath. A soft noise came from just outside the door. It wasn't footsteps—it sounded more like fabric gently brushing against the wood. Then it stopped.

Trying to stay calm, Sorelli walked toward the door. Her voice trembled a bit as she asked,

"Who's there?"

No answer.

All eyes were on her, so she took a deep breath and said louder,

"Is someone there?"

"Yes! Of course, there is!" Meg Giry shouted, yanking on Sorelli's skirt. "Don't open it! Please don't open the door!"

But Sorelli, who always carried a small dagger, unlocked the door and pulled it open while the rest of the girls hurried into the back of the room. Meg whispered,

"Mother... please..."

Sorelli peeked into the hallway. It was empty. A single gaslight flickered behind its glass cover, casting a weak, reddish glow that couldn't fully light the space. The shadows seemed to stretch endlessly. Sorelli closed the door and sighed.

"No one's there," she said.

"But we saw him!" Jammes insisted as she slowly came back to stand beside Sorelli. "He's still out there, hiding. I'm not getting dressed again. Let's all go downstairs together for the speech and come back up together too."

She gently touched her small coral ring—a charm she believed brought good luck. Sorelli, trying not to show she was nervous, lightly traced a cross on the wooden ring she wore on her left hand.

"Come on, girls," she said, "get yourselves together. No one's actually seen the ghost."

"Yes, we have!" the girls shouted. "We just saw him! He had the same skull face and black suit that Joseph Buquet talked about!"

"And Gabriel saw him yesterday!" added Jammes. "In the afternoon! In broad daylight!"

"Gabriel—the chorus master?"

"Yes! Didn't you know?"

"Wait… you're saying the ghost was wearing a tuxedo in the daytime?"

"Who, Gabriel?"

"No! The ghost!"

"Obviously! That's how Gabriel recognized him," Jammes said.

Gabriel had been in the stage manager's office when the Persian showed up.

"You know," Jammes whispered, "people say the Persian has the evil eye…"

"Oh yes!" the girls all agreed at once. Then, just to be safe, they quickly made the hand gesture to keep bad luck away—index and pinky fingers out, with the others bent down and held by the thumb—just in case the Persian really could curse someone.

"You all know how superstitious Gabriel is," Jammes went on. "But he's always polite. Whenever he sees the Persian, he puts his hand in his pocket and touches his keys for good luck. Well, when the Persian suddenly showed up in the doorway, Gabriel jumped straight from his chair to the cabinet—so he could touch something made of iron. In the rush, he ripped the entire bottom of his coat on a nail. Then he hit his head on a hook, leaving a giant bump. He backed up, scraped his arm on the edge of a screen, and when he tried to steady himself on the piano, the lid slammed down on his fingers. He ran out like he'd gone crazy, slipped on the stairs, and fell down the whole first flight on his back. I happened to be passing by with Mother, and we helped him up. He was all bruised and his face was covered in blood.

We were terrified. But then, all of a sudden, he thanked heaven that it hadn't been worse. That's when he told us what had scared him—he saw the ghost behind the Persian! The same ghost Joseph Buquet described, with the skull face!"

Jammes had rushed through her story like she thought the ghost was right behind her, and by the time she finished, she was out of breath. The room fell quiet. Sorelli nervously filed her nails while the girls processed what they'd just heard. Then little Giry spoke up:

"Joseph Buquet should've kept quiet."

"Why?" someone asked.

"That's what my mom thinks," Meg answered softly, glancing around the room like she was afraid someone might be listening.

"Why does she think that?"

"Shhh! Mom says the ghost doesn't like it when people talk about him."

"How does she know?"

"Because—because... never mind."

That vague answer only made the girls more curious. They crowded around Meg, begging her to explain. All of them leaned in at once, nervous but excited, their fear feeding off one another. Somehow, being scared together made the whole thing feel even more real—and a little thrilling.

"I swore I wouldn't say anything!" Meg whispered.

But the others wouldn't let it go. They promised to keep it a secret until finally, Meg, itching to share what she knew, gave in. Her eyes stayed locked on the door as she began:

"It's because of the private box."

"What box?"

"The ghost's box."

"The ghost has a box? Tell us! Please!"

"Not so loud," Meg warned. "It's Box Five—you know, the one next to the stage box, on the left side of the grand tier."

"Oh, come on!"

"I swear it's true. My mom takes care of it. But you have to promise not to tell anyone."

"Of course, we promise!"

"Well, that's the ghost's box. No one's been allowed to sit there for over a month—except the ghost. The box office has orders to never sell it."

"And the ghost actually goes there?"

"Yes."

"So... someone really sits there?"

"No. The ghost does—but the seat stays empty."

The girls looked at each other, confused. If the ghost really sat there, they should've seen him—especially if he wore a black suit and had a skull for a face, like everyone said. They tried to explain this to Meg, but she shook her head.

"That's just it. No one sees him. He doesn't have a tuxedo or a skull face. All that stuff about a flaming head or skeleton is made up. You don't see him—you only hear him. My mom's never seen him, but she's definitely heard him. She knows he's there because she gives him his program."

Sorelli cut in.

"Giry, you're making this up."

Little Giry's eyes filled with tears.

"I should've kept quiet. If my mom finds out I told, she'll be furious. But I'm telling you, she was right. Joseph Buquet should've kept his mouth shut. She said he'd get into trouble for talking about things that don't concern him… she said it just last night…"

Suddenly, heavy footsteps pounded down the hallway. A breathless voice called out:

"Cecile! Cecile! Are you in there?"

"It's my mom!" Jammes said and rushed to open the door.

A large, serious-looking woman stormed into the room, clearly upset. She dropped into the nearest chair, gasping. Her face was flushed, and her eyes looked wild.

"It's terrible," she said, "just awful!"

"What is? What happened?"

"It's Joseph Buquet."

"What about him?"

"He's dead!"

The room exploded with shocked gasps and questions.

"They found him hanging… in the third-floor basement."

"It's the ghost!" little Giry blurted out before she could stop herself. Then, covering her mouth with both hands, she quickly added, "No, no! I didn't say that—I didn't say anything!"

Around her, the other girls, frozen with fear, whispered the same thought:

"Yes… it has to be the ghost."

Sorelli's face had gone pale.

"I'll never be able to give my speech now," she muttered.

Madame Jammes gave her own opinion while downing a glass of liqueur she found on a nearby table. She was sure the ghost had something to do with what had happened.

The truth is, no one really knew how Joseph Buquet died. The official report said it was suicide. In his Memoirs of a Manager, M. Moncharmin—one of the two new managers who took over after Debienne and Poligny—wrote about the event like this:

"A terrible accident ruined the farewell party that MM. Debienne and Poligny hosted to celebrate their retirement. I was in my office when Mercier, the acting manager, burst in looking completely frantic. He told me a stagehand had been found hanging in the third basement under the stage—right between a farmhouse set and a backdrop from The King of Lahore. I shouted,

'Come on! We have to cut him down!'

But by the time we got down the stairs and climbed down the ladder, the man wasn't hanging anymore. He was gone."

And that's what M. Moncharmin considered normal. A man found hanging from a rope, and when they rush to save him, the rope has vanished. But Moncharmin had a simple explanation:

"It happened right after the ballet," he said, "and the dancers wasted no time protecting themselves from bad luck."

So, in other words, the ballet girls supposedly rushed down, cut the rope, and took pieces of it as charms—just like that.

But when I think about where Joseph's body was found—way down in the third basement under the stage—I can't help but feel like someone wanted that rope gone. Someone had a reason to make sure it disappeared after it served its purpose. Maybe time will prove me right.

News of the awful event spread quickly through the Opera. Joseph Buquet had been well-liked, and everyone was shocked. Dressing rooms emptied out fast, and the ballet girls gathered tightly around Sorelli like frightened lambs clinging to their shepherd. They hurried through the dim hallways and down the staircases, their little pink legs moving as fast as they could carry them.

Chapter II
The New Margarita

On the first landing of the stairs, Sorelli bumped into the Comte de Chagny, who was heading up. He was usually calm and collected, but now he looked excited.

"I was just on my way to find you," he said, taking off his hat. "Sorelli, what a night! And Christine Daaé—what a performance!"

"That's impossible!" said Meg Giry. "Just six months ago, she sang like a total beginner!" Then, with a playful curtsy, she added, "But please move aside, dear Count. We're going to check on a poor man who was found hanging."

At that moment, the acting manager came rushing by and stopped when he heard what Meg said.

"What?" he snapped. "You girls already heard? Please, forget it for now. And whatever you do, don't let Messrs. Debienne and Poligny find out—it would ruin their last night here."

They all continued to the ballet foyer, which was already packed. The Count was right—no farewell event had ever been as grand as this one. Several famous composers had taken turns conducting their own music. Faure and Krauss had sung. And that night, Christine Daaé finally revealed her full talent to an audience that was shocked and thrilled.

Gounod conducted the Funeral March of a Marionette; Reyer led his beautiful Overture to Sigurd; Saint-Saëns conducted both Danse Macabre and Reverie Orientale; Massenet presented a new Hungarian march; Guiraud conducted Carnaval; and Delibes brought out the Valse Lente from Sylvia and the Pizzicati from Coppélia. Mlle. Krauss performed the bolero from I Vespri Siciliani, and Mlle. Denise Bloch sang the drinking song from Lucrezia Borgia.

But the biggest moment of the night belonged to Christine Daaé. She started with a few parts from Romeo and Juliet. It was her first time singing in this Gounod opera, which had never been performed at the main Opera House but had once been staged by Mme. Carvalho at the Théâtre Lyrique. People said Christine's voice sounded angelic— but that was nothing compared to what she did later in the prison scene and the final trio from Faust. She filled in for La Carlotta, who was out sick, and the audience was stunned. No one had ever heard anything like it.

That night, Christine became a whole new Margarita on stage— shining and full of life, in a way no one expected. The crowd went wild, jumping to their feet, shouting, clapping, cheering. Christine broke down in tears, fainted, and had to be carried to her dressing room by the other singers.

Still, some longtime audience members were frustrated. Why had someone with a voice like hers been kept hidden until now? Until that night, Christine had only played Siebel, a small part beside Carlotta's dramatic and bold Margarita. And it took Carlotta's sudden and strange absence for Christine to finally get her moment to shine.

Now, everyone wanted answers: Why did the managers choose Christine as the backup? Did they already know how talented she really was? If so, why keep her in the background? And if they didn't know, how did she suddenly become so amazing? Even more curious— Christine wasn't known to have a singing teacher at that time. She had said more than once that she planned to train on her own from now on. The whole thing felt like a mystery.

Meanwhile, the Comte de Chagny watched it all from his box, fully caught up in the excitement, clapping along with everyone else. His full name was Philippe Georges Marie, Comte de Chagny, and he was forty-one years old. He was tall, good-looking, and had an elegant air about him, though his expression was often serious and his eyes a bit cold. He was extremely polite to women but a bit distant with other men, who sometimes resented how well he did in high society. Still, Philippe had a good heart and strong morals.

When his father, the old Count Philibert, passed away, Philippe became the head of one of the oldest and most respected families in France—going back to the 1300s. The Chagny family owned a lot of land and wealth. After his father, a widower, died, Philippe took over managing everything, which was no small task. His two sisters and younger brother, Raoul, didn't argue about splitting the estate. They fully trusted Philippe to handle it all, as if the old tradition of the oldest son inheriting everything still held true. When the two sisters got married on the same day, Philippe gave them their share—not because they demanded it, but as wedding gifts, which they accepted with thanks.

The Comtesse de Chagny, formerly known as Miss de Moerogis de La Martyniere, died giving birth to Raoul, who was born twenty years after his older brother. When their father passed away, Raoul was only twelve years old. From then on, Philippe took charge of raising and educating him. His sisters helped at first, and later, an older aunt—whose husband had been a naval officer—continued his care. She lived in Brest and sparked Raoul's love for the sea.

Raoul joined the naval training ship Borda, graduated with honors, and even completed a trip around the world. With strong support from high places, he was recently chosen to join an official mission aboard the ship Requin. They were going to the Arctic to look for survivors from the D'Artoi expedition, which had been missing for three years. But before setting sail, Raoul was given a long break—six months of leave. During this time, the older women in Paris society were already feeling sorry for him, thinking that such a handsome and gentle young man wouldn't last long in such a tough job.

Raoul was shy—almost innocent. He acted like he had just stepped away from being raised by women, which wasn't far from the truth. Having grown up surrounded by his sisters and his aunt, he developed soft manners and a sweet charm that nothing had yet ruined. He had just turned twenty-one but looked more like he was eighteen. With light blonde hair, kind blue eyes, a soft mustache, and smooth skin, he looked more like a young woman than a sailor.

Philippe adored Raoul and was incredibly proud of him. He believed Raoul had a bright future in the navy, just like their ancestor Chagny de La Roche, who had once been an admiral. While Raoul was on leave, Philippe took him around Paris, introducing him to its elegant and artistic world. Philippe believed that at Raoul's age, it wasn't healthy to be too perfect or too sheltered. He himself had always balanced responsibility and fun, always behaved properly, and never set a bad example for his brother. He brought Raoul with him everywhere, even to the ballet foyer.

Some people gossiped about Philippe's friendly relationship with the dancer Sorelli, but it wasn't something shocking. He was a wealthy, unmarried man with free time—especially now that his sisters were married—so spending a couple of hours after dinner with a pretty dancer wasn't unusual. Sorelli wasn't particularly witty, but she had the most beautiful eyes in Paris. Besides, a true Parisian nobleman like the Comte de Chagny was expected to be seen at places like the Opera's ballet foyer, which was one of the most fashionable spots at the time.

Still, Philippe probably wouldn't have brought Raoul behind the scenes if Raoul hadn't begged to go. He asked over and over, and Philippe remembered that later.

That evening, after the crowd went wild for Christine Daaé, Philippe looked at Raoul and noticed his face was pale.

"Don't you see?" Raoul said. "She fainted!"

"You look like you're about to faint yourself," Philippe replied. "What's going on with you?"

But Raoul had already pulled himself together and stood up.

"Let's go check on her," he said. "She's never sung like that before."

Philippe gave his brother a knowing smile and didn't say a word. They walked toward the passage that led from the audience area to the stage, where lots of other guests were slowly making their way. Raoul, lost in thought, nervously tore his gloves without noticing. Philippe, with his kind heart, didn't tease him, but he finally understood why Raoul had seemed so distracted lately—and why he always changed the subject to the Opera.

They made their way to the stage, moving through a crowd of men, crew members, and chorus girls. Raoul led the way, his face serious and full of emotion, as if something inside him had changed. Philippe followed behind, still smiling to himself.

At the back of the stage, Raoul was stopped by a group of ballet girls crowding the hallway he wanted to get through. Some of them called out teasing comments with painted lips, but he ignored them. Eventually, he slipped past and entered a dim hallway filled with the sound of people calling out:

"Daaé! Daaé!"

Philippe was surprised that Raoul knew exactly where he was going. He'd never personally taken him to visit Christine. That meant Raoul had gone there on his own—probably while Philippe was talking with Sorelli, who often asked him to wait backstage until her performance. Sometimes, she even gave him her little over-shoes to carry—ones she wore to protect her satin dance shoes and her tights as she hurried from her dressing room.

Sorelli had her reasons. She had lost her mother.

Delaying his usual stop by Sorelli's dressing room, the Count followed Raoul down the hallway to Christine Daaé's room. He saw that it had never been so packed—everyone in the theater seemed excited by Christine's incredible performance and also worried about her sudden fainting. She still hadn't woken up. The theater's doctor had just arrived, walking in right behind Raoul. Christine slowly opened her eyes while being helped by the doctor—though it was in Raoul's arms that she first woke up.

The Count and many others stood in the doorway, crowding to get a look.

"There's no air in here," Raoul said calmly. "Doctor, don't you think it's time these gentlemen cleared out?"

"You're absolutely right," the doctor replied.

He asked everyone to leave, allowing only Raoul and Christine's maid to stay. The maid looked at Raoul with wide, curious eyes—she had never seen him before, but she didn't dare question him. The doctor assumed Raoul must have some right to be there and let it go.

So the young Viscount stayed, quietly watching Christine as she slowly came back to herself. Even the two managers, Debienne and Poligny, who had come to offer congratulations, were left standing out in the hallway with the other well-dressed guests.

From the crowd, the Count de Chagny chuckled.

"Ah, clever boy," he whispered to himself. "These young men with their innocent faces... so, he really is a Chagny."

He turned to go see Sorelli but ran into her on the way, surrounded by the nervous group of ballet girls, just as described earlier.

Inside the dressing room, Christine let out a deep sigh, which was answered by a quiet groan. She turned her head, saw Raoul, and jumped slightly. She glanced at the doctor, smiling faintly, then at her maid, then back at Raoul.

"Sir," she whispered, "who are you?"

"Mademoiselle," Raoul answered, kneeling down and kissing her hand with deep emotion, "I'm the little boy who jumped into the sea to save your scarf."

Christine looked again at the doctor and the maid—and the three of them burst into soft laughter.

Raoul's face turned bright red as he stood up.

"Since you're pretending not to know me, Mademoiselle," he said, trying to sound serious, "I'd like to speak to you alone. It's important."

"Maybe later... when I'm feeling better?" she said, her voice trembling slightly. "You've been very kind."

"Yes, you should go now," the doctor added with a warm smile. "Let me take care of her."

"I'm fine now," Christine said suddenly, her voice stronger and more determined.

She stood up and gently rubbed her eyelids.

"Thank you, Doctor. I'd like to be alone. Please, all of you, go. I can't sit still tonight. I need space."

The doctor began to protest, but after seeing how unsettled she was, he decided it was better not to argue. As he left, he said to Raoul in a low voice:

"She's not herself tonight. Normally she's so calm and sweet."

Then the doctor said good night, and Raoul was left alone. This part of the theater was now completely quiet. Most people had likely gone to the farewell celebration in the ballet foyer. Raoul guessed Christine might join them, so he waited, standing quietly in the shadows of a nearby doorway. His heart ached with emotion, and he needed to talk to her right away.

Suddenly, the door to the dressing room opened and Christine's maid stepped out, carrying a few bundles. Raoul stopped her and asked how Christine was doing. The woman laughed and said Christine was perfectly fine—but didn't want to be disturbed. She said Christine had asked to be left alone, then walked away.

Only one thought filled Raoul's mind:

She wanted to be alone for him!

Didn't she know he had asked to speak with her privately?

Raoul walked quietly up to Christine's dressing room, barely breathing. He raised his hand to knock but stopped, pressing his ear to the door to listen first. Just then, he heard a deep, commanding voice from inside:

"Christine, you must love me!"

Christine replied, her voice soft and shaky, like she was crying:

"How can you say that? I sing only for you!"

Raoul leaned against the wall, overwhelmed. His heart, which had felt completely empty just moments before, was now pounding so hard he thought the sound might echo down the hallway. It filled his ears, and he feared the people inside might hear it, open the door, and catch him listening. That would be humiliating—especially for someone from a noble family like his. He pressed his hands to his chest, as if trying to quiet the sound.

Then the man spoke again:

"Are you very tired?"

Christine answered:

"Tonight, I gave you my soul… and now I feel like I've died."

"Your soul is a beautiful thing," the man said gently. "Thank you. No emperor has ever received such a gift. The angels wept tonight."

After that, Raoul couldn't hear anything else. But still, he didn't leave. Hiding in the shadows, he stayed, determined to see who the man was. In that moment, he truly understood what love and jealousy felt like. He knew without a doubt that he loved Christine. Now he needed to know who he was up against.

To his shock, the door opened—and Christine stepped out by herself. She was wrapped in a warm coat, her face hidden by a lace veil. She closed the door quietly, but Raoul noticed she didn't lock it. She walked right past him without seeing him. He didn't even move or turn to follow her. He only stared at the door, which stayed shut.

When the hallway was empty, he walked over and slipped inside. He closed the door behind him. The room was pitch black. Someone had turned off the gas lights.

"Someone's here," Raoul said, his voice trembling. His back was still pressed against the door. "Why are you hiding?"

There was no reply. The silence felt heavy. All he could hear was his own breathing. He didn't even stop to think how wrong it was for him to be in there alone.

"You're not leaving until I say you can," he yelled. "If you don't answer me, you're a coward. I'll tell everyone about you!"

He struck a match. The small flame lit the room—

No one was there.

Quickly, he locked the door and turned on the gas lamps. He searched everywhere—inside closets, behind curtains, even ran his hands along the walls. But he found nothing.

"Am I going crazy?" he said out loud.

He stood there for ten minutes, just listening to the soft hiss of the gaslight in the still room. Even though he was madly in love, he didn't even think of taking a scarf or glove to feel close to Christine. At last, he stepped out, lost in thought and unsure of where he was going.

As he wandered through the theater, a cold gust of air brushed his face. He looked up and realized he was at the bottom of a staircase. Behind him, a group of stagehands was walking by, carrying a stretcher covered by a white sheet.

"Excuse me, which way is the exit?" Raoul asked one of them.

"Straight ahead," the man said. "Door's open. But let us through first."

Without thinking, Raoul pointed at the stretcher. "What happened? Who is that?"

One of the workers answered:

"That's Joseph Buquet. They found him hanging in the third basement—between a farmhouse set and part of The King of Lahore scene."

Raoul slowly took off his hat, stepped aside to let them pass, and quietly walked out.

Chapter III
The Mysterious Reason

While all this was going on, the farewell party was in full swing. As mentioned before, the event was being held in honor of M. Debienne and M. Poligny, who had decided to retire in style. They wanted to leave on a high note, and thanks to help from many important people in Paris's social and artistic circles, their big night was going exactly as planned—even if it was a bit sad.

After the performance, everyone gathered in the ballet foyer. Sorelli stood near the entrance, holding a glass of champagne and ready to give a short speech she had prepared. Behind her, the ballet dancers— both younger and older—whispered about the events of the evening or exchanged quiet glances and signals with their friends, many of whom were gathered noisily around the long tables filled with food and drinks.

A few dancers had already changed into their regular clothes, but most of them still wore their delicate ballet skirts made of thin gauze. They had all made an effort to look extra polished for the occasion— everyone, that is, except for little Jammes. At just fifteen, she had already managed to push thoughts of the ghost and Joseph Buquet's death out of her mind. She couldn't stop laughing, jumping around, making jokes, and teasing her friends—until the moment Debienne and Poligny appeared at the top of the steps. Sorelli, clearly annoyed, scolded her sharply.

People noticed right away that the two managers looked unusually cheerful. That's typical for Parisians, though. In Paris, people often hide their real feelings. If someone is heartbroken, they'll smile like everything's fine. If they're lucky or happy, they may act bored or even annoyed. Life in the city is like a never-ending masquerade. And for two smart men like Debienne and Poligny, the ballet foyer was the last place they'd show how emotional they really were. They smiled a little too widely as Sorelli began her speech.

But suddenly, little Jammes let out a scream that cut through the noise and completely broke the mood:

"The Opera ghost!"

She pointed into the crowd. Everyone turned to look at a pale, frightening face, with sunken black eyes and a ghastly expression. The man looked so much like a skeleton that it shocked the whole room.

"The Opera ghost! The Opera ghost!" she cried.

People laughed nervously, nudged each other, and joked about buying the ghost a drink—but he had already vanished. He slipped away into the crowd, and no one could find him, even though many tried. Meanwhile, two older men tried to calm Jammes down, and little Giry started shrieking like a bird.

Sorelli was furious. She never got to finish her speech. The managers gave her a quick kiss on the cheek, thanked her, and disappeared just as quickly as the ghost.

No one was really surprised. Everyone knew they had more appearances to make—one upstairs in the singers' foyer and one final gathering with close friends in the grand lobby near the managers' offices, where a proper supper was waiting.

In the grand lobby, the guests found the new managers, M. Armand Moncharmin and M. Firmin Richard. They barely knew these men, but still greeted them warmly, showering them with compliments. The new managers returned the favor with flattery of their own, and the guests, who had expected a dull evening, began to enjoy themselves. The mood lifted, and the atmosphere turned cheerful. A witty speech from a government official, who praised both the Opera's rich history and its bright future, made everyone even more relaxed and friendly.

The former managers, Debienne and Poligny, had already given their successors the two tiny master keys that opened every door in the Opera House—thousands of doors in total. These little keys sparked curiosity and were passed around the table from guest to guest. But then something caught the attention of a few people near the far end of the table.

There, sitting quietly, was a strange, pale man with sunken eyes— the same terrifying face that had been seen earlier in the ballet foyer when little Jammes had screamed:

"The Opera ghost!"

The man looked perfectly real, just like anyone else—except that he didn't eat or drink. At first, people smiled when they looked at him, thinking it was some sort of joke. But soon, their smiles faded. His presence was unsettling. No one laughed, and no one dared repeat the joke from earlier. No one said:

"There's the Opera ghost!"

The man didn't say a word, and no one sitting next to him could say exactly when he had joined them. But everyone had the same eerie feeling: if the dead ever came to dine with the living, they would look just like this man.

Some of the guests assumed he must have come with the old managers, while others thought he was a guest of the new ones. Because of this, no one asked who he was. No one wanted to say something rude that might offend him. A few people who had heard rumors about the ghost—and remembered how the stagehand had described him—began to wonder if this really was the ghost. They didn't yet know about Joseph Buquet's death. The only thing that didn't match was that the ghost was said to have no nose, and this man did.

Still, Moncharmin later wrote in his memoirs that the man's nose was strange—"long, thin, and transparent," he said. Maybe it was a fake nose, shiny enough to look see-through. After all, fake noses made by doctors can look very real.

So, did the Opera ghost actually sit at the managers' dinner that night, completely uninvited? Was it really him? No one could say for sure. I'm not sharing this to make you believe he had the nerve to crash the party—but simply because the whole thing, while strange, truly happened.

Moncharmin even wrote in his memoirs:

"When I think back on that first night, I can't separate the secret that Debienne and Poligny shared with us from the presence of that ghostly figure at our dinner table—the one none of us recognized."

Here's what happened: Debienne and Poligny were sitting near the middle of the table and hadn't noticed the strange man yet. But suddenly, he spoke.

"The ballet girls are right," he said. "That poor Buquet's death might not be as natural as everyone thinks."

Debienne and Poligny turned sharply toward him.

"Buquet is dead?" they gasped.

"Yes," the man replied calmly. "He was found this evening, hanging in the third basement, between a farmhouse backdrop and a scene from The King of Lahore."

The two former managers stood up quickly and stared at the man who had just spoken. They looked more shocked than they should have been, especially since the news was simply about a stagehand's death. Both turned pale—paler than the white tablecloth in front of them. Debienne gave a quick signal to the new managers, Richard and Moncharmin, while Poligny mumbled an excuse to the guests. Then, the four of them left the dinner and headed into the managers' office.

M. Moncharmin picks up the story from here in his memoirs:

"Debienne and Poligny seemed increasingly nervous, like they had something difficult to tell us. First, they asked if we knew the man who told them about Joseph Buquet's death—the one sitting at the end of the table. When we said no, they looked even more troubled.

They took the master keys from us, stared at them for a moment, and suggested we change the locks—quietly and without drawing attention—on any rooms or closets we wanted to keep secure. The way they said it sounded so strange, we couldn't help but laugh. We asked if there were thieves in the Opera.

They said no, it was something worse—the ghost.

We laughed again, thinking this was part of some elaborate joke to make the night more entertaining. At their request, we tried to act serious and play along. That's when they told us they never would have brought up the ghost if they hadn't received specific instructions from him to do so. He had told them to be kind to him and to give him whatever he asked for.

Still, they admitted they had put off telling us until the very last minute, hoping they could just walk away without sharing the strange truth. But the news of Buquet's death reminded them of how badly things could go when the ghost didn't get his way. Whenever they ignored him, something awful or bizarre would happen—something that always forced them to listen to him again.

While they were saying all this in hushed and serious voices, I looked at Richard. Back in school, he had a reputation for playing pranks, and now it looked like he was enjoying having the tables turned. He listened carefully to every word, even though the whole thing was starting to sound like a creepy story.

He nodded slowly and acted like he already regretted ever agreeing to run the Opera. I copied his serious expression, just to go along with the moment. But in the end, we couldn't help it—we burst out laughing. We laughed so hard, right in Debienne and Poligny's faces, that they stared at us like we'd gone completely crazy.

The joke was wearing thin. Richard, trying to keep things moving, asked with a half-serious, half-joking tone:

'So what does this ghost of yours actually want?'

Poligny walked over to his desk and came back with a copy of the Opera's official agreement—the document that lists the terms under which someone can manage the Opera. It started with the usual promise to keep the Opera shining as the best musical stage in France and ended with Clause 98, which said that the agreement could be canceled if the manager broke any of the conditions.

There were four usual rules written in the contract. But the version Poligny handed us had something added at the end. It was a new paragraph written in red ink, with shaky, uneven letters—like someone had used the tip of a matchstick to write it. The handwriting looked like it belonged to a child who hadn't yet learned how to write properly. The extra line said:

"5. Or if the manager is ever more than two weeks late in paying the Opera ghost's monthly allowance—which is twenty thousand francs a month, or two hundred and forty thousand francs a year."

Poligny pointed to that part, clearly uneasy.

Richard, keeping his cool, asked,

"Is that all? Doesn't he want anything else?"

"Actually, he does," Poligny replied.

He turned the pages until he found the section about the private opera boxes reserved for special guests like the president and other government leaders. At the end of that section, another sentence had been added in the same red, scratchy handwriting:

"Box Five, on the grand tier, must be reserved for the Opera ghost at every performance."

When we saw that note, all we could do was get up from our seats, shake hands with Debienne and Poligny, and thank them for pulling such a clever prank. It really showed that the classic French sense of humor was still alive and well. Richard even joked that now he finally understood why they were stepping down from running the Opera—because no one could do business with such a demanding ghost.

"Of course, you don't just find two hundred and forty thousand francs lying around," said Poligny, completely serious. "And did you think about how much money we lost because of Box Five? We couldn't sell it even once! And not only that—we had to refund the subscription. It's ridiculous. We're not here to support ghosts. That's why we're leaving."

"Yes," added Debienne, "we're better off walking away. Let's go."

And he stood up.

Richard replied, "Honestly, I think you were way too nice to the ghost. If I had a ghost causing that much trouble, I'd just have him arrested."

"Arrested? But how? Where?" they both asked at once. "We've never even seen him!"

"But what about when he's in his box?"

"We've never seen him there, either!"

"Then sell the box," Richard said.

"Sell the ghost's box? Gentlemen, go ahead and try."

With that, all four of us left the office. Richard and I had never laughed so hard in our lives.

Chapter IV
Box Five

Armand Moncharmin wrote such a long set of memoirs during his time running the Opera that it's hard to imagine he had time to actually manage anything besides writing about it. He didn't know a thing about music, but he was friendly with the Minister of Education and Fine Arts, had written a few articles for society newspapers, and came from a wealthy family. He was a likable guy and showed he wasn't lacking in common sense—because once he decided to be more of a behind-the-scenes partner at the Opera, he chose a strong leader to handle the day-to-day work: Firmin Richard.

Firmin Richard was a respected composer. He had written many popular pieces and enjoyed all types of music and musicians. Because of that, most musicians liked him in return. The only downsides were that he liked things his way and had a bit of a quick temper.

During their first few days in charge of the Opera, both men were thrilled to be running such an impressive place. They had completely forgotten the strange story of the Opera ghost—until something happened that reminded them it wasn't over.

That morning, Firmin Richard arrived at his office around eleven. His secretary, M. Remy, handed him a few unopened letters marked "private." One of them immediately caught Richard's attention—not just because the address was written in red ink, but because the handwriting looked oddly familiar. He soon realized it matched the red ink writing in the contract where the ghost's demands had been added.

It had the same awkward, messy look—like a child who hadn't learned how to write neatly.

He opened the letter and read:

DEAR MR. MANAGER,

I'm sorry to bother you while you're probably very busy renewing contracts, making new ones, and showing off your excellent taste. I know you've helped Carlotta, Sorelli, little Jammes, and others whose talents you've either guessed or confirmed.

Of course, when I say "talents," I'm not talking about La Carlotta, who sings like a leaky watering can and should've stayed at the Ambassadeurs or Café Jacquin. I'm not talking about Sorelli, who owes her success more to the carriage makers than her dancing. And I'm definitely not talking about little Jammes, who dances like a clumsy baby cow.

And I'm also not talking about Christine Daaé—even though she's truly gifted. But because you're jealous of her, you're not letting her have any real roles. That's your business, I suppose. You can run things however you want.

Still, I'd like to ask for one small favor. Since you haven't fired Christine Daaé yet, I'd like to hear her sing tonight in the role of Siebel, since you banned her from singing Margarita after her incredible performance the other night. Also, please don't give away my box today—or any day going forward. I have to tell you I've been quite annoyed to find out more than once that my box was sold at your order when I arrived at the Opera.

I didn't complain right away because I don't like causing drama. I also thought Debienne and Poligny had simply forgotten to tell you about my little preferences before they left. But now I've received their reply to my letter, and they confirmed you know all about the special conditions written in the Memorandum-Book. That means you're treating me with serious disrespect.

If you want peace, don't take away my box.

Sincerely,

Your Most Humble and Obedient Servant,

THE OPERA GHOST

The letter also included a clipped message from the "agony column" of the Revue Théâtrale newspaper. It read:

O.G.—There's no excuse for R. and M. We told them and gave them your Memo. Best wishes.

Firmin Richard had just finished reading the letter when Moncharmin walked in, holding an identical one. They looked at each other and burst out laughing.

"They're really keeping this joke going," said Richard. "But I don't find it funny."

"What are they trying to do?" asked Moncharmin. "Do they think they can keep a box forever just because they used to run the Opera?"

"I'm not in the mood to be made fun of," said Richard.

"Still," said Moncharmin, "it's harmless. All they want is the box for tonight, right?"

Richard told his secretary to send Box Five to Debienne and Poligny if it hadn't already been sold. It hadn't, so it was sent. Debienne lived at the corner of Rue Scribe and Boulevard des Capucines, and Poligny lived on Rue Auber. Moncharmin noted that both letters had been mailed from the post office on Boulevard des Capucines.

"See what I mean?" said Richard.

They both shrugged and shook their heads, disappointed that two grown men could waste time on silly games like this.

"They could've at least been polite about it," said Moncharmin. "Did you notice how rude they were about Carlotta, Sorelli, and little Jammes?"

"My dear friend, those two are just jealous!" said Richard. "Can you believe they even paid for an ad in the Revue Théâtrale? Don't they have anything better to do?"

Moncharmin nodded. "They seem oddly focused on that little Christine Daaé."

"You know she has a solid reputation," Richard replied.

"Reputations are easy to get," said Moncharmin. "People say I know all about music, and I don't even know the difference between two notes."

"Don't worry—you've never had that reputation," Richard said, laughing.

Then, he told his assistant to send in the performers who had been waiting for hours outside the door—nervous, pacing, hoping for a shot at success… or fearing rejection.

The rest of the day was packed with auditions, contract talks, signings, and cancellations. Exhausted, the two new managers went to bed early and didn't even bother checking Box Five to see whether Debienne and Poligny had attended the show.

The next morning, a card arrived from the Opera ghost:

DEAR MR. MANAGER,

Thanks. Lovely evening. Daaé was wonderful. The chorus needs more energy. Carlotta is a fine instrument, but dull.

I'll write again soon about the 240,000 francs—or to be exact, 233,424 francs and 70 centimes. Debienne and Poligny have already sent me the 6,575 francs and 30 centimes for the first ten days of this year. Their time in charge ended on the 10th.

Best wishes,

O.G.

There was also a letter from Debienne and Poligny:

GENTLEMEN,

Thank you for your kind gesture, but you must understand that, as former managers, even if we'd enjoy hearing Faust again, we have no right to sit in Box Five on the grand tier. That box belongs to the person we discussed with you when we went through the memorandum-book. Please see Clause 98, final paragraph.

Sincerely,

Debienne and Poligny

"This is getting ridiculous!" Richard shouted, grabbing the letter.

That evening, they sold Box Five.

The next morning, Richard and Moncharmin arrived at the office and found a report from one of the Opera's inspectors. It described something that had happened in Box Five the night before. Here's the key part:

I had to call for a guard twice to clear out Box Five. Once at the beginning of the show, and once again in the middle of Act Two. The people in the box were laughing loudly and making silly comments.

People around them kept shouting, "Shhh!" and the whole audience was getting upset. The box-keeper came to get me. I went to the box, warned the guests, and told them to keep quiet. They seemed a little off and said strange things. I told them if the noise continued, they'd be removed.

As soon as I left, they started laughing again. I brought back a guard, and we made them leave. They protested and said they wouldn't go unless they got their money back. Eventually, they calmed down and were allowed to return. But the moment they sat down, they started laughing again, so we removed them for good.

"Send for the inspector," Richard said to his secretary, who had already marked the report with a blue pencil.

M. Remy had expected the request and called the inspector in right away.

"Explain what happened," Richard said sharply.

The inspector fumbled through the report, then said, "Sir, I think they'd been drinking. They didn't seem interested in the show at all. The moment they went into the box, they came back out and told the box-keeper, 'Take a look inside—there's no one in there, right?' She said, 'No, it's empty.' Then they told her, 'Well, when we stepped in, we heard a voice say the box was already taken!'"

Moncharmin couldn't help but smile and glanced at Richard—but Richard didn't smile back. He knew this kind of prank too well. In his younger days, he'd pulled similar tricks, and he recognized the signs: what starts off funny quickly becomes irritating.

Trying to get on Moncharmin's good side, the inspector let out a small chuckle.

Big mistake.

Richard glared at him, and from that point on, the inspector kept a completely serious, almost terrified expression on his face.

"But when those people got to the box," Richard shouted, "there was no one in it, right?"

"Not a single person, sir, not one! Not in that box, or the one next to it on either side. Completely empty, I swear! The box-keeper told me that herself many times—it just proves it was all a joke."

"Oh, so you do think it was a joke?" Richard snapped. "And I suppose you found it funny?"

"No, sir. I thought it was in very poor taste."

"And what did the box-keeper say?"

"She just said it was the Opera ghost. That's all."

The inspector grinned, but it was a mistake. The moment those words left his mouth, Richard's annoyed expression turned to full-blown anger.

"Send for the box-keeper!" he shouted. "Right now! And get those people out of here!"

The inspector started to object, but Richard cut him off with a sharp order to stay quiet. After a moment of silence, Richard glared and demanded:

"Well? Who is this 'Opera ghost'?"

The inspector, now too nervous to speak, threw up his hands in a helpless gesture to show he didn't know—or didn't want to know.

"Have you ever seen him?" Richard demanded. "Have you ever actually seen the Opera ghost?"

The inspector shook his head firmly—no, he hadn't.

"Very well," said Richard coldly.

The inspector's eyes widened in panic, as if to say, Why did he say it like that?

"Because," Richard said, "I'm going to start holding people responsible if they haven't seen him. If this ghost is always around, then I'm not going to accept people claiming they've never seen him. When I hire someone, I expect them to do their job!"

With that, Richard turned away and began talking business with his acting manager, who had just walked into the office. The inspector, thinking it was safe to leave, started quietly edging toward the door.

"Stay where you are!" Richard bellowed, freezing the man in place.

Meanwhile, Remy had already sent someone to get the box-keeper from the Rue de Provence, where she worked as a porter. Soon, she walked into the room.

"What's your name?" Richard asked.

"Madame Giry. You know me, sir. I'm the mother of little Giry— Meg, remember?"

She said this in a proud, dramatic tone. For a moment, Richard was almost impressed. He looked her over: faded shawl, worn-out shoes, old dress, and a dull bonnet. It was clear he either didn't know her or didn't remember her—or Meg. But Mme. Giry was so proud that she assumed everyone knew who she was.

"Never heard of her," Richard said. "But that doesn't mean I can't ask what happened last night that made you and the inspector bring in a police guard."

"I've been wanting to talk to you about that, sir," she replied. "I didn't want you to run into the same trouble as Messieurs Debienne and Poligny. They didn't listen to me either—not at first."

"I'm not asking about all that," Richard interrupted. "I'm asking what happened last night."

Mme. Giry turned red with anger. No one had ever spoken to her that way before. She stood up stiffly, smoothed out her skirt, and lifted her head proudly, making the feathers in her worn bonnet bob. But then she changed her mind, sat back down, and said in a stern voice:

"I'll tell you what happened. The ghost was upset again."

Just as Richard was about to explode with anger, Moncharmin stepped in and took over the questioning. From what they could tell, Mme. Giry didn't find it strange at all that a voice could be heard in a box that was completely empty. To her, this was just the Opera ghost doing what he always did. No one ever saw him, but people often heard him. She herself had heard him many times. And they could trust her, she said, because she always told the truth. They could ask Debienne, Poligny, or anyone who knew her—including Isidore Saack, who had supposedly had his leg broken by the ghost.

"Really?" said Moncharmin, raising an eyebrow. "The ghost broke Saack's leg?"

Mme. Giry looked shocked, as if surprised they didn't already know. Still, she was willing to explain what had happened to these two "poor clueless men." She said it happened back when Debienne and Poligny were in charge—also in Box Five—during a performance of Faust.

Mme. Giry cleared her throat as though she were about to sing the entire opera herself, then began:

"It happened like this, sir. That night, Monsieur Maniera and his wife—you know, the jewelers from Rue Mogador—were sitting in the front seats of the box. With them was their close friend, Monsieur Isidore Saack, sitting just behind Madame Maniera.

Mephistopheles was singing,"—Mme. Giry suddenly broke into song—'Catarina, while you play at sleeping'—"when M. Maniera heard a voice whisper in his right ear, 'Ha, ha! Julie's not pretending to sleep!' His wife's name was Julie. So he turned to his right to see who had said it—but no one was there. He rubbed his ear, wondering if he imagined it. Then Mephistopheles continued his song…

"Oh, I'm not boring you, am I?"

"No, not at all. Please go on."

"You're too kind," she said with a proud smile. "So Mephistopheles went on,"—and she sang again—'Saint, unclose thy portals holy…'—"and again M. Maniera heard the voice in his ear: 'Ha, ha! Julie wouldn't mind giving Isidore a kiss!' This time, he turned to the left—and guess what he saw?

Isidore was holding Julie's hand and kissing it through the little hole in her glove—like this." Mme. Giry acted it out by kissing the palm of her own glove with great drama. "Then all chaos broke loose! Bang! Bang! M. Maniera, who was a big, strong man like you, Monsieur Richard, punched poor Isidore, who was small and thin, more like Monsieur Moncharmin—no offense! The shouting started, people in the audience were yelling, 'Stop them! He'll kill him!' And finally, Isidore ran off."

"So the ghost didn't actually break his leg?" Moncharmin asked, a bit annoyed that she had compared him to the smaller man.

"Oh, but he did, sir," she said, lifting her chin proudly. "He broke it on the grand staircase—Isidore was running away so fast, he tumbled right down, and it'll be a long time before he walks up those steps again!"

"And did the ghost tell you what he whispered in Maniera's ear?" Moncharmin asked, pretending to be serious but clearly amused.

"No, sir—that part came from M. Maniera himself."

"But you've actually spoken to the ghost yourself?"

"As clearly as I'm speaking to you now, sir."

"And what does he say when he talks to you?"

"He usually tells me to bring him a footstool."

At that, Richard burst out laughing, and Moncharmin and their secretary, Remy, joined in. Only the inspector stayed quiet—he had already learned not to laugh at anything involving the ghost. Mme. Giry, however, puffed up with anger and gave them all a look of pure offense.

"Instead of laughing," she said sternly, "you should do what M. Poligny did. He went and found out for himself!"

"Found out what?" asked Moncharmin, who was now fully entertained.

"About the ghost, of course!"

She suddenly grew serious, as if preparing for a dramatic moment.

"Listen," she said. "They were performing La Juive. M. Poligny decided to watch the show from the ghost's box. So when the scene came where Léopold cries, 'Let us fly!' and Eléazar stops him and says, 'Where are you going?'—well, M. Poligny..."

She paused, eyes wide, as if what came next would change everything.

"...I was watching from the next box, which was empty, and I saw it all."

Poligny stood up and left the box stiffly, like a statue. Before I could even ask him, "Where are you going?"—like in the play—he was already down the stairs. Luckily, he didn't break his leg.

"But that still doesn't explain how the Opera ghost asked you for a footstool," Moncharmin said.

"Well," replied Mme. Giry, "after that night, no one ever tried to take the ghost's box again. The manager gave orders to always keep it reserved for him. And every time the ghost came to the opera, he'd ask me for a footstool."

"A ghost asking for a footstool?" Moncharmin scoffed. "What is he—a woman?"

"No, the ghost is a man."

"How do you know that?"

"Because he has a man's voice. Oh, it's such a beautiful voice! This is what happens: He usually shows up during the first act. He knocks three times on the door of Box Five. The first time I heard those taps—knowing the box was empty—I was very confused. I opened the door, looked around—no one there. Then I heard a voice say, 'Mme. Jules'—my poor husband's name was Jules—'a footstool, please.' I'll be honest, it gave me a strange feeling. But then the voice said, 'Don't be afraid, Mme. Jules, I'm the Opera ghost!' And his voice was so gentle and kind, I wasn't even scared. The voice was coming from the front-right chair in the box."

"Was anyone in the box next to it?" asked Moncharmin.

"No, sir. Box Seven on the right and Box Three on the left were both empty. The show had just started."

"And what did you do?"

"I brought the footstool, of course. It wasn't for him—it was for the lady he was with. But I never saw her or heard her speak."

"What? So now the ghost has a wife?" The two managers turned to glance at the inspector, who was standing behind Mme. Giry, trying to get their attention. He tapped his finger to his temple in a silent gesture to suggest that Mme. Giry was clearly out of her mind. Richard saw this and made up his mind to fire the inspector for keeping "a crazy woman" on the staff.

Meanwhile, Mme. Giry kept going, now talking about how generous the ghost could be:

"After the show, he always left me money—two francs, sometimes five, even ten if he hadn't been around in a while. But now that people are bothering him again, he doesn't leave me anything."

"Excuse me, madam," Moncharmin said (Mme. Giry frowned at his overly familiar tone), "how exactly does the ghost give you this money?"

"He leaves it on the little shelf in the box," she replied. "I always leave the program there for him, and I find the money next to it. Sometimes there are even flowers—like a rose, probably from his lady's dress. Once, they even left a fan behind."

"Oh? The ghost left a fan?" Richard asked. "What did you do with it?"

"I brought it back the next night," she said simply.

At that point, the inspector cut in, "That's against the rules. I'll have to fine you, Mme. Giry."

"Shut up, you fool," Richard muttered under his breath.

"You brought the fan back. Then what?" Moncharmin asked.

"They took it," she said. "At the end of the performance, it was gone. But in its place, they left me a box of English candies. I love English sweets. That was one of the ghost's sweet little gestures."

"That's enough, Mme. Giry. You may go now."

Mme. Giry gave a proud, dignified nod and left the room like royalty. After she was gone, the manager told the inspector they would no longer need her services. When the inspector also left, they told the acting manager to begin processing the inspector's termination as well.

Once they were alone, Richard and Moncharmin shared a look. They were both thinking the same thing: it was time they investigated Box Five themselves.

Chapter V
The Enchanted Violin

Christine Daaé didn't continue her rise at the Opera right away, and there were reasons for that—though they'll be explained later. After her big night on stage, she sang one more time at a private event hosted by the Duchess de Zurich. But after that, no one heard her perform in private again. She even backed out of a charity concert she had promised to attend, and she didn't give any real reason why. It was as if she no longer had control over her own choices, like she was scared of succeeding too much.

She knew the Comte de Chagny had spoken to M. Richard about her, trying to help her on behalf of his younger brother. Christine wrote to thank him but also asked him not to speak for her again. No one ever really understood why she did that. Some people said she was being too proud. Others believed she was just shy and humble. But people in show business usually aren't that modest. It seemed more likely that she was afraid. Yes—afraid of something that had happened.

There's a letter she wrote around that time (which is now in the Persian's collection) that shows just how shaken she was. In it, she says, "I don't know myself when I sing." That short line says everything—she didn't even recognize herself anymore.

She avoided people, and the Vicomte de Chagny kept trying to see her. He wrote letters, asked to visit, but got no answer. Just when he was about to give up, she finally sent him a note:

Monsieur:

I haven't forgotten the little boy who jumped into the sea to save my scarf. I feel like I need to write to you today. I'm going to Perros to keep a sacred promise. Tomorrow is the anniversary of my dear father's death. You knew him, and he cared for you very much. He's buried there, with his violin, in the churchyard at the bottom of the hill where we used to play as children. It's also near the road where we said goodbye for the last time.

As soon as Raoul read the letter, he rushed to find a train schedule, quickly got dressed, scribbled a note for his brother, and jumped in a cab to the train station. But he arrived just too late and missed the morning train. He spent the rest of the day feeling frustrated and down.

That night, he finally boarded the train to Brittany. As he rode through the darkness, his mood began to lift. He read Christine's note over and over again, breathing in the scent of the paper, and remembering their childhood. The long ride passed in a mix of happy memories and hopeful dreams—each one starting and ending with Christine.

At sunrise, he got off the train in Lannion and took a coach to Perros-Guirec. He was the only passenger. He talked to the driver and found out that the day before, a young woman who looked like she was from Paris had arrived in Perros. She was staying at an inn called The Setting Sun.

As Raoul got closer, he started thinking more about Christine's past—memories most people didn't know.

Christine had been born in a small town near Uppsala, Sweden. Her father was a poor farmer during the week and sang in church on Sundays. He taught Christine music before she could even read. He might not have realized it, but he was a gifted musician—one of the best violinists in all of Scandinavia. People everywhere asked him to play at weddings and festivals. When Christine was around six years old, her mother passed away. After that, her father sold their land, took Christine with him, and moved to Uppsala to chase a better life through music.

But instead of finding success, all he found was poverty.

He went back to the countryside, moving from fair to fair, playing his old Scandinavian tunes. Christine, who never left his side, would listen with joy or sing along while he played. One day at the Ljimby Fair, a man named Professor Valerius heard them perform and was so impressed that he brought them to the city of Gothenburg. He said Christine's father was the best violinist in the world and believed Christine could become a great singer. He helped pay for her education and music lessons. Christine quickly improved and won everyone over with her charm, sweet personality, and eagerness to learn.

Later, when Professor Valerius and his wife moved to France, they brought Daaé and Christine with them. "Mamma" Valerius treated Christine like her own daughter. But her father became homesick. He barely went outside in Paris. Instead, he spent most of his time in his room with Christine, playing his violin and singing softly. Sometimes, Mamma Valerius would quietly listen outside the door, wipe away a tear, and tiptoe back downstairs, missing the skies of her homeland.

Daaé didn't begin to feel better until summer, when the family took a trip to Perros-Guirec, a quiet seaside town in Brittany. The sea there was the same color as in his home country, and it brought him comfort. He would often sit on the beach and play his saddest songs, pretending the sea stopped to listen. He also convinced Mamma Valerius to let him do something a little unusual. During the local festivals and religious events known as "pardons," he took Christine with him for a week, like in the old days, traveling from village to village with his fiddle.

They brought music to even the tiniest towns, sleeping in barns and refusing beds at inns. They wore neat clothes and never accepted money, even when people offered.

The townspeople were curious about the quiet man and his pretty daughter who sang like an angel. They followed them from one village to the next.

One day, a young boy out walking with his governess made her take a longer walk than planned because he couldn't stop listening to Christine's beautiful singing. They ended up at a quiet beach called Trestraou—though now it's home to a casino or something like that. Back then, it was just sky, sea, and golden sand. A strong wind picked up and blew Christine's scarf out over the water. She cried out and reached for it, but it was already far out at sea.

Then, she heard a boy's voice say,

"Don't worry—I'll get your scarf!"

She turned and saw the same little boy running toward the waves, even though his governess, a serious lady in black, shouted for him to stop. But he didn't listen—he ran straight into the water, clothes and all, and brought the scarf back. Both he and the scarf were soaking wet. The governess scolded him, but Christine just laughed and kissed the boy in thanks.

That little boy was Raoul, the Vicomte de Chagny. He was staying nearby in Lannion with his aunt.

All through that summer, Raoul and Christine saw each other and played together almost every day. His aunt, along with Professor Valerius, asked Daaé to give Raoul some violin lessons. During those lessons, Raoul learned to love the same songs that had filled Christine's childhood. The two of them were quiet, thoughtful kids who loved listening to stories and fairy tales. Their favorite game was going from house to house asking the elderly folks for old legends, saying:

"Excuse me, ma'am…" or "Kind sir, do you have a story you could tell us?"

And almost always, they got one. In Brittany, many older people had stories to share—about magical creatures like the "korrigans," who were said to dance in the moonlight on the moors.

But their favorite moments came at twilight. After the sun dipped into the sea, Daaé would sit with them by the side of the road and, in a quiet voice—as if he didn't want to scare away the spirits—he would tell them tales from the North.

As soon as he finished one story, the children would beg for another.

One of their favorite stories started like this:

"A king sat in a small boat on a still, deep lake that looked like a shining eye among the mountains of Norway..."

And there was another story they loved just as much...

Little Lotte was a girl who dreamed about everything and nothing. Her hair was as bright as sunlight, and her soul was as clear and blue as her eyes. She was sweet to her mother, gentle with her doll, careful with her dress, her red shoes, and her violin. But most of all, she loved listening to the Angel of Music before falling asleep.

As Christine's father told this story, Raoul couldn't help but stare at her golden hair and bright blue eyes. Christine, meanwhile, thought Lotte was lucky to hear the Angel sing her to sleep. The Angel of Music was part of all Daddy Daaé's stories. He believed that every truly great musician or artist would hear from the Angel at least once in their life.

Sometimes the Angel would visit them as babies, like Lotte, and those children would grow up to play music better than adults ever could. Other times, the Angel would come later—if the child was stubborn or didn't want to practice. And sometimes, the Angel never came at all, especially if the child had a bad heart or a guilty conscience.

No one ever saw the Angel, but those chosen to hear him would suddenly be surrounded by heavenly music, a beautiful voice they would remember forever. These special people could sing or play in a way that made all other music seem dull. People would call them geniuses, not knowing the Angel had paid them a visit.

One day, little Christine asked her father if he had ever heard the Angel. He sadly shook his head, but then his eyes lit up and he said,

"One day, you will, my child! When I'm in Heaven, I'll send him to you."

By then, Daddy Daaé had already begun to cough a lot.

Three years later, Christine and Raoul saw each other again in Perros. Professor Valerius had passed away, but his widow was still in France with Christine and her father. The two of them filled the house with music, and Mamma Valerius, who now lived only for that music, was happy just listening.

Raoul, now a grown man, had come to Perros hoping to find them. He went straight to the house where they used to stay. First, he saw Christine's father. Then Christine walked in with a tray of tea. She blushed when she saw Raoul. He went up and kissed her gently. Christine asked him a few polite questions, served the tea, and then left the room. But outside, she sat down in the garden, her heart full of feelings she hadn't known before.

Raoul followed her, and they spent the rest of the day talking quietly and carefully, trying not to show how nervous they were. When it was time to say goodbye, Raoul kissed her hand and said,

"Mademoiselle, I will never forget you."

But he regretted those words right away. He knew that a girl like Christine could never marry someone like the Vicomte de Chagny.

Christine, on the other hand, tried hard not to think about Raoul. She threw herself into her music and made amazing progress. People who heard her sing said she would become one of the greatest performers in the world.

Then her father died—and it was like she lost her voice, her joy, and her spark all at once. She still had just enough talent to enter the Conservatoire, a top music school, but she didn't shine. She went through the motions only to make Mamma Valerius happy. The woman had taken her in like a second mother, and Christine continued to live with her.

When Raoul first saw Christine again at the Opera, he was stunned by her beauty and flooded with memories. But he was confused by how dull her singing had become. He kept coming back to watch her, trying to catch her attention backstage or near her box. He even followed her after performances. But Christine never noticed him. She didn't seem to notice anyone. She acted like she was in a world of her own.

Raoul was hurt. She was so beautiful, and he was too shy to admit he loved her—even to himself.

Then came that unforgettable night at the gala performance. Everything changed. Her voice soared like an angel's, shaking the heavens. That moment won Raoul's heart completely.

And then… there was that deep, strange voice Raoul had heard through the door—"You must love me!"—even though the room had seemed completely empty…

Why had Christine laughed when he brought up the memory of the scarf? Why had she acted like she didn't even know him? And if she really didn't, why had she sent him a letter?

Finally, Raoul arrived in Perros. He stepped into the dim, smoky sitting room of the inn called The Setting Sun, and right away, he saw Christine standing there. She smiled softly, as if she had expected him.

"So, you came," she said. "I had a feeling I'd see you here after I got back from church. Someone told me I would."

"Who told you?" Raoul asked as he gently took her hand.

"My father," she said quietly, "my poor father who passed away."

There was a long silence. Then Raoul asked in a soft voice,

"Did your father also tell you that I love you, Christine? That I can't live without you?"

Christine's cheeks turned bright red. She looked away and said, her voice unsteady,

"Me? You must be imagining things, my friend!"

Then she gave a shaky laugh, like she was trying to make light of the moment.

"Please don't laugh, Christine. I'm being serious," Raoul said.

Christine's smile faded. She looked at him with a more serious expression and said,

"That's not why I wrote to you."

"But you did write to me," Raoul said, not letting it go. "You had to know your letter would bring me here. Why would you do that, unless you knew I cared about you?"

"I just thought maybe you'd remember how we used to play here when we were kids... how my father always played with us. Honestly, I'm not sure why I wrote to you. Maybe it was just the date... maybe seeing you again at the Opera brought everything back. For a moment, I felt like that little girl again."

There was something in her tone, something about the way she acted, that felt off to Raoul. She wasn't being mean—he could see she still cared. But there was a sadness in her, and he didn't understand why.

"Was that really the first time you noticed me—when I came into your dressing room?" he asked.

Christine didn't try to lie.

"No," she said softly. "I'd seen you before. In your brother's box... and once from the stage."

"I thought so!" Raoul said, clenching his fists. "Then why, when I stood there reminding you about the scarf and our childhood, did you act like you didn't remember me? Why did you laugh?"

He hadn't meant to sound angry, but his voice came out harsh. Christine looked at him, startled. Raoul was shocked at himself too. He had meant to be gentle—to tell her how much he cared. But instead, he sounded like a jealous husband scolding a wife. He knew he'd gone too far, but now he didn't know how to take it back.

"You won't answer?" he said bitterly. "Fine. I'll say it for you. You acted like that because someone else was in your dressing room— someone you didn't want to know that you cared about anyone else!"

Christine's voice went cold.

"If anyone was in my way that night, Raoul, it was you. I asked you to leave, didn't I?"

"Yes! So you could be alone with him!" Raoul snapped.

"What are you talking about?" Christine said sharply. "Who do you think was with me?"

"The man you told: 'I sing only for you... tonight I gave you my soul, and now I'm dead!'"

At that, Christine grabbed his arm tightly—stronger than he ever would've guessed someone like her could be.

"So you were spying on me? Listening at the door?"

"Yes," Raoul admitted, heart pounding. "Because I love you... and I heard everything."

"Heard what exactly?" Christine asked, suddenly calm again. She slowly let go of his arm.

"He told you, 'Christine, you must love me!'"

When Raoul said those words, Christine's face turned pale like she had seen a ghost. Dark shadows appeared under her eyes, and she looked like she might faint. Raoul rushed to catch her, but she steadied herself just in time. In a soft voice, she said,

"Go on. Keep talking. Tell me everything you heard."

Still confused and shaken, Raoul said,

"I heard him answer you after you told him you gave him your soul. He said, 'Your soul is a beautiful thing, child, and I thank you. No emperor has ever received such a gift. The angels cried tonight.'"

Christine put her hand over her heart, clearly overwhelmed. Her eyes stared ahead like she was in a trance. Raoul was scared—she looked like she wasn't fully there. Slowly, tears formed in her eyes and rolled down her cheeks like pearls.

"Christine!"

"Raoul!"

He reached for her, wanting to hold her, but she pulled away and ran out of the room in a panic.

She locked herself in her room, and Raoul didn't know what to do. He was too upset to eat breakfast. He had hoped for a warm, happy time with her, but the hours dragged by with no sign of Christine.

Why wouldn't she come out and walk with him through the countryside, the same paths they used to explore as kids? He heard that she went to church early that morning, had a special mass said for her father, and spent time praying at his grave. But if she was finished with that, why stay in Perros doing nothing instead of returning to Paris?

Feeling sad and restless, Raoul wandered to the church graveyard. He walked alone between the graves, reading the names on the tombstones. Then, behind the church, something bright caught his eye. It was a bunch of red roses blooming in the snow—bright and full of life right in the middle of a place full of death. Skulls and bones were stacked against the church wall, held in place with wire. They looked like bricks, forming the base of the sacristy wall. The doorway to the sacristy was built right into this creepy wall, which was common in old Breton churches.

Raoul said a quiet prayer for Christine's father, Daaé. Then, disturbed by the eerie sight of all those grinning skulls, he climbed up a small hill and sat on the edge, looking out at the sea. The wind had died down. It was cold and dark, but he didn't feel it.

This was the spot where he and Christine used to sit as kids, watching for the Korrigans—magical creatures from local stories. Raoul had never seen any, even though his eyesight was sharp. Christine, who couldn't see very far, always swore she saw them dancing in the moonlight. He smiled at the memory—until a voice behind him made him jump.

"Do you think the Korrigans will come tonight?"

It was Christine.

Raoul tried to say something, but Christine gently placed her gloved hand over his mouth.

"Listen, Raoul. I need to tell you something really serious. Do you remember the story about the Angel of Music?"

"Of course," he said. "Your father told us that story right here."

"And do you remember when he said, 'When I'm in Heaven, my child, I will send him to you'? Well, Raoul, my father is in Heaven now... and the Angel of Music has come to me."

"I believe you," Raoul replied quietly. He thought she was just remembering her father in a sweet and symbolic way, especially after her incredible singing performance.

But Christine looked surprised by how calmly he took it.

"How do you understand what I'm saying?" she asked, leaning in so close he thought she might kiss him—but she was just trying to see his expression through the darkness.

"I understand," Raoul said, "that no one could sing the way you did the other night without help from something beyond this world.

No teacher could have taught you that. You've really heard the Angel of Music, Christine."

"Yes," Christine said seriously. "He comes to my dressing room every day to give me music lessons."

"In your dressing room?" Raoul repeated, surprised.

"Yes, that's where I've heard him. And I'm not the only one who has."

"Who else heard him, Christine?"

"You did, Raoul."

"Me? I heard the Angel of Music?"

"Yes. That night, when you were listening outside my door—it was him speaking. He was the one who said, 'You must love me.' I thought I was the only one who could hear him. So when you said this morning that you'd heard him too, I was shocked."

Raoul laughed. The moonlight was starting to shine down on them, casting a soft glow. Christine suddenly looked angry. Her gentle eyes flashed with frustration.

"Why are you laughing? Do you think you just heard some random man's voice?"

"Well..." Raoul said, his thoughts becoming a bit scrambled by how serious Christine was.

"It's you, Raoul! We've known each other since we were little! You were my father's friend! How can you even think that I'd secretly let a man into my dressing room? I'm an honest girl. If you had opened the door, you would've seen no one was there."

"That's true," Raoul said. "I did open the door after you left... and the room was empty."

"Exactly," Christine replied. "So?"

Raoul took a deep breath and said, "Christine, I think someone's tricking you."

Christine gasped and suddenly ran away. Raoul tried to catch up, but she shouted, "Leave me! Just go!" Then she was gone.

Raoul returned to the inn feeling tired, upset, and heartbroken. The staff told him Christine had gone up to her room and wouldn't be coming down for dinner. He ate alone, feeling gloomy. Later, he tried reading, then went to bed, but couldn't sleep. Everything was quiet next door.

Time passed slowly. Around 11:30, Raoul clearly heard soft footsteps in the room next to his. Christine hadn't gone to bed. He didn't know what made him do it, but he got dressed quietly and waited. His heart was beating fast. Then, Christine's door creaked open.

Where could she be going at this hour, when the whole town was asleep?

He opened his own door carefully and saw Christine, glowing in the moonlight, walking silently down the hall. She went down the stairs. Raoul leaned over the railing to watch. Then, he heard two voices talking quickly. One sentence stood out: "Don't lose the key." It was the landlady. The front door, which faced the sea, opened and shut.

Silence.

Raoul rushed back into his room and opened his window. He saw Christine standing alone on the empty dock.

The second floor wasn't very high, and there was a tree nearby. Its branches reached toward his window, so Raoul climbed down without being seen.

That's why the landlady was so shocked the next morning when someone found Raoul lying on the church steps—freezing and barely conscious. He was brought back to the inn, half-frozen. The landlady ran to tell Christine, who came right away to help. With her and the landlady's care, Raoul slowly woke up and smiled when he saw Christine's face looking down at him.

A few weeks later, something terrible happened at the Opera, and a police investigation began. The officer, M. Mifroid, questioned Raoul about what happened that night in Perros. Here's part of the official report:

Q: "Did Mademoiselle Daaé see you climbing down from your room in such a strange way?"

A: "No, sir, she didn't. I didn't try to be quiet when I followed her. In fact, I hoped she would notice me. I knew I had no right to spy on her like that—it wasn't right—but I couldn't help myself. Still, she acted like I wasn't there. She left the dock calmly, then suddenly started walking faster. When the church clock struck 11:45, I thought that was why she was in such a hurry. She ran and didn't stop until she got to the church."

Q: "Was the gate open?"

A: "Yes, sir. I was surprised it was open, but Christine didn't seem to think anything of it."

Q: "Was anyone else in the churchyard?"

A: "No, sir. I didn't see anyone. And I would've, if they were there. The moonlight was bright, and the snow made it easy to see everything."

Q: "Could someone have hidden behind the gravestones?"

A: "No. The gravestones were small and mostly buried in snow. Only the tops of the crosses showed. There weren't many places to hide. The church and yard were clear, and the shadows came only from the crosses and from us. The night was cold and clear—you could see everything plainly."

Q: "Are you superstitious?"

A: "No, sir. I'm a practicing Catholic."

Q: "What were you feeling that night?"

A: "I was calm and in a good state of mind. At first, I was worried when Christine left the inn so late, but when I saw her heading to the graveyard, I figured she was visiting her father's grave. That made sense, so I relaxed. I was only surprised she didn't notice I was walking behind her—my footsteps were loud on the icy snow. But I figured she was just deep in thought, and I didn't want to disturb her. She knelt at the grave, crossed herself, and started praying. Then, right as the clock struck midnight, she looked up at the sky and raised her arms like she was in a trance. I didn't know what was happening, until I looked up too—and suddenly, I heard the most beautiful music."

"It was a tune Christine and I knew from when we were kids, but this time, it sounded more perfect than ever—better even than how her father used to play it. I remembered Christine's stories about the Angel of Music. The song was The Resurrection of Lazarus, something her father often played during quiet, emotional moments. If the Angel of Music was real, that's exactly how he would've played it—on her father's old violin. When the music stopped, I thought I heard something strange, like the skulls nearby were laughing. It gave me chills."

Q: "Did you think someone could be hiding behind the pile of bones?"

A: "Yes, sir, that's exactly what I thought. I became so focused on that idea that I didn't notice Christine walking away. She was moving slowly and didn't see me at all."

Q: "So how did you end up found passed out on the church altar the next morning?"

A: "A skull rolled to my feet… then another… and another. It was like someone was tossing them at me, like it was a creepy game. I thought whoever was hiding behind the bones had accidentally knocked them over. That idea made sense when I saw a shadow moving along the church wall. I ran after it. The figure opened the door to the church and slipped inside. I was faster and managed to grab the edge of its cloak."

"We stopped right in front of the altar. The moonlight came through the stained-glass windows and lit us both up. I held onto the cloak, and the figure turned around. I saw a terrifying skull-like face with eyes that burned right into me. It felt like I was staring at the devil himself. I completely froze. I fainted. After that, I remember nothing— until I woke up at the inn."

Chapter VI
A Visit to Box Five

We left M. Firmin Richard and M. Armand Moncharmin just as they were deciding to "check out Box Five."

They walked away from the grand staircase that leads from the managers' offices to the stage. They crossed the stage, exited through the door used by subscribers, and entered the theater through a nearby hallway. Then they made their way through the front rows of seats to look at Box Five on the grand tier. They couldn't see it very well—it was half in the dark and covered, like the rest of the boxes, with heavy cloths draped over the red velvet.

The Opera House was almost completely empty and silent. Most of the stage crew had stepped out for a drink. The set was halfway finished, and the stage was quiet and still. A few dim, eerie beams of light—like the last light from a dying star—shone on a cardboard tower that had fake stone walls. In that strange light, everything looked dreamlike and odd.

The seats in the orchestra section were covered with cloth that, in the gloom, looked like a frozen green sea. Moncharmin and Richard were like shipwrecked sailors wading through this strange ocean, struggling toward the left side of the theater. Huge pillars stood like cliffs, and the layered balconies above them looked like rocky waves ready to collapse. High above, painted figures on the ceiling seemed to laugh and mock the two men as they stared up. These were supposed to be serious mythological characters—like Isis, Amphitrite, Pandora, and Galatea—but under the flickering light, even they looked like they were having fun at the managers' expense.

Finally, the two men grabbed onto the edge of a box, as if holding on to wreckage from a shipwreck, and stared at Box Five.

They were clearly unsettled. At least Moncharmin admits he was. In his memoirs, he wrote:

"All this nonsense about the Opera Ghost, which we'd been hearing about since taking over from Debienne and Poligny, must've messed with my head. Maybe the spooky atmosphere in the empty theater had gotten to us. Maybe we imagined things in the half-light of Box Five. But I swear, I saw something—and Richard saw it too. We didn't say a word, just grabbed each other's hands and stood frozen, staring at the same spot. Then the figure disappeared. Later, when we talked in the hallway, we realized that we'd both seen something different. I saw a skull resting on the ledge. Richard saw what looked like old Madame Giry. We figured out that we'd both been tricked by our imagination."

Laughing nervously, they ran to Box Five. They went inside and found absolutely nothing strange.

Box Five was no different than any other grand-tier box. Same red velvet, same chairs, same carpet. They checked every chair, especially the one where the mysterious "man's voice" was said to sit—but it was just a regular, fancy seat. They even felt the carpet like detectives, but there was nothing hidden there or anywhere else.

Then they checked the box directly underneath—Box Five on the lower tier—but still, nothing.

"These people are making fools of us!" Firmin Richard finally said. "They're playing games. Faust is showing on Saturday—we'll both watch from Box Five!"

Chapter VII
Faust and What Followed

On Saturday morning, when the two managers arrived at their office, they found a letter from O.G. It said:

Dear Managers,

So, this means war?

If you still want peace, here are my conditions—take them or leave them:

1. Give me back my private box. I want to use it whenever I please.

2. Christine Daaé must sing the role of Margarita tonight. Don't worry about Carlotta—she'll be sick.

3. I demand that Madame Giry, my box-keeper, be immediately returned to her job.

4. Send me a letter, through Madame Giry, confirming that you accept the terms in my memorandum regarding my monthly payment. I'll explain later how you're supposed to pay me.

5. If you refuse, then be warned—tonight's performance of Faust will take place in a cursed theater.

Take my advice while there's still time.

– O.G.

"I'm sick of him! Completely sick of him!" Richard shouted, slamming his fists on the desk.

Just then, Mercier, the acting manager, walked in.

"Lachenel wants to see one of you right away," he said. "He says it's urgent, and he looks pretty upset."

"Who's Lachenel?" asked Richard.

"He's your head groom."

"My what?"

"Your head groom, sir," Mercier explained. "There are several grooms who work at the Opera, and Lachenel is in charge of them."

"What does he do exactly?"

"He runs the stables."

"Stables? There are stables in the Opera?"

"Yes, sir—under the building, near the Rotunda side. It's an important department. We keep twelve horses down there."

"Twelve horses! What on earth for?"

"For stage performances," Mercier said. "We need trained horses for shows like La Juive and The Prophet. The grooms train them to stay calm and behave onstage. Lachenel is really good at it—he used to manage the horses at Franconi's circus."

"Okay, fine. But what does he want now?"

"I'm not sure, sir. But I've never seen him this upset."

"Let him in."

Lachenel entered, holding a riding crop and smacking it against his boot in frustration.

"Good morning, Mr. Lachenel," said Richard, a little taken aback. "What brings you here?"

"Sir, I'm here to ask you to get rid of the entire stable staff."

"What—you want us to fire the horses?"

"No, not the horses. The men who work in the stables."

"How many do you have?" asked Richard.

"Six," Lachenel replied. "That's at least two too many."

Mercier spoke up, "Those jobs were assigned by the under-secretary of fine arts. They're government appointees, and if I may—"

"I don't care about the government!" Richard snapped. "We don't need more than four men to care for twelve horses."

"Eleven," Lachenel corrected.

"Twelve!" Richard barked back.

"Eleven," Lachenel repeated.

"Oh, but the acting manager told me there were twelve horses!" said Richard.

"There were twelve," Lachenel said. "But now I only have eleven. César was stolen."

He angrily smacked his boot with his riding crop.

"César's been stolen?" the acting manager shouted. "César—the white horse from The Prophet?"

"There's only one César," Lachenel said firmly. "I worked ten years with Franconi's stables, and I've seen hundreds of horses. But there's no other horse like César. And now he's gone."

"How did it happen?"

"I don't know. No one does. That's why I'm here—to tell you to fire the whole stable staff."

"What do your stablemen say?"

"They're all blaming each other. Some say it was the stagehands. Others think it was the acting manager's doorman."

"My doorman?" Mercier said, shocked. "I trust him completely—just like I trust myself!"

"But surely you have some idea what happened," Richard said.

"I do," Lachenel said, stepping closer to the managers. "And I'll tell you what it is. I have no doubt in my mind." He leaned in and whispered, "It was the ghost who took César!"

Richard jumped to his feet. "What? Not you too!"

"What do you mean, 'me too'? Isn't it obvious? Especially after what I saw?"

"What did you see?"

"I saw a black figure riding a white horse—César—clear as day."

"Did you chase them?"

"I did. I even yelled. But they were too fast. They vanished into the dark tunnels under the building."

Richard stood up. "That's enough, Mr. Lachenel. You can leave now. We'll file a complaint against this ghost of yours."

"And what about my stable staff? Will you fire them?"

"Of course! Goodbye."

Lachenel bowed and left the room. Richard was fuming.

"Settle his account right away. I want him gone."

"But sir," Mercier said, "he's friends with the government official..."

"And he drinks vermouth at Tortoni's with Lagrene, Scholl, and Pertuiset—the lion hunter," added Moncharmin. "If we fire him, the whole press will turn on us. He'll spread ghost stories, and people will laugh at us! We'll be a joke!"

"Fine, just drop it for now."

At that moment, the door suddenly opened. The person who usually stood guard must've been missing, because Madame Giry walked right in without knocking. She held a letter in her hand and spoke quickly:

"Excuse me, gentlemen. I just received a letter from the Opera Ghost. He told me to come see you, that you had something—"

She didn't finish. She saw Richard's face and froze. He looked furious—too angry to speak. And then, without warning, he exploded.

First, he grabbed Madame Giry by the arm and spun her halfway around. She let out a surprised, frightened scream. Then, he kicked her so hard that her long black skirt flew up behind her. It all happened so fast that Madame Giry didn't know what had hit her until she found herself outside the office, completely stunned. And then, she did understand. Her angry voice echoed through the Opera House as she screamed, protested, and shouted threats.

Meanwhile, at her home in the Rue du Faubourg Saint-Honoré, Carlotta was still in bed when her maid brought her the morning's letters. One of them was anonymous, written in red ink in shaky, clumsy handwriting. It said:

If you sing tonight, be ready for something terrible to happen the moment you open your mouth... something worse than death.

Carlotta lost her appetite for breakfast after reading the letter. She pushed her cup of hot chocolate away, sat up in bed, and thought hard. It wasn't the first time she had gotten a threatening note, but this one felt much more serious than the others.

At the time, Carlotta believed she was the target of jealous people trying to ruin her. She told everyone she had a secret enemy plotting against her, but also claimed she wasn't the kind of woman to be scared off easily.

In reality, if there was a plot, Carlotta herself was behind it—against poor Christine, who didn't suspect a thing. Carlotta had never forgiven Christine for the night she stepped in at the last minute and gave a performance that amazed everyone. The moment Carlotta heard about Christine's success, she suddenly felt better—her sore throat and anger at the Opera's managers magically disappeared—and she made sure not to miss another show. From then on, she did everything she could to outshine Christine. She called in favors from powerful friends to convince the managers not to give Christine more chances to perform. Even the newspapers that once praised Christine suddenly focused only on Carlotta. Inside the Opera, Carlotta—famous but cold-hearted—made rude comments about Christine and tried to make her life difficult.

After finishing the threatening letter, Carlotta got out of bed and said, "We'll see about that," swearing angrily in Spanish, determined not to be scared.

The first thing she saw when she looked out the window was a hearse. Being very superstitious, the sight of it, combined with the letter, made her feel like something bad really might happen that night. She quickly gathered her supporters and told them Christine was behind a plot to ruin her. Carlotta told them they needed to teach Christine a lesson by filling the Opera House with people who supported her. Carlotta wasn't short on fans, and she expected them to be ready for anything—to cheer loudly for her and stop any troublemakers.

Later, M. Richard's secretary visited to check on her health. He brought a message from the manager, advising her to rest, avoid cold air, and stay home until the evening. Carlotta said she was perfectly fine and that even if she were dying, she would still sing the role of Margarita that night. After he left, she couldn't help but think how strange it was to be told to stay inside—right after receiving a threatening letter.

At five o'clock, another anonymous note arrived. It was in the same messy red handwriting as the first. This one was shorter and read:

You have a bad cold. If you're smart, you'll realize it's madness to try and sing tonight.

Carlotta laughed, tossed her head, and sang a few lines to prove her voice was just fine.

That night, her loyal fans showed up to support her. They watched the crowd carefully but saw no sign of any troublemakers. The only odd thing was that both M. Richard and M. Moncharmin were sitting in Box Five—the one that supposedly belonged to the Opera Ghost. Carlotta's fans guessed that maybe the managers had also heard about a planned protest and had come to deal with it in person. But in truth, as the reader knows, the two managers were only there to see if the ghost would appear.

Meanwhile, the opera began. The famous baritone, Carolus Fonta, had just finished Dr. Faust's first big moment on stage:

"In vain I cry out in this long night,

No answer comes from the heavens' height!"

As the applause faded, M. Richard, seated in the front chair of Box Five—the ghost's usual seat—leaned toward Moncharmin and joked:

"Well, has the ghost whispered anything to you yet?"

Moncharmin laughed. "Not yet. Don't be so impatient. The show just started. The ghost usually shows up during the first act, not before."

The first act ended without anything unusual happening. But Carlotta's fans weren't surprised—after all, her character, Margarita, didn't sing in that act. When the curtain came down, the two managers glanced at each other… still waiting.

"That's one act down," Moncharmin said.

"Yes, and the ghost is running late," Richard replied with a grin.

"Not a bad crowd tonight," Moncharmin added. "Especially for a theater that's supposed to be cursed."

Richard chuckled and pointed to a woman sitting in the middle of the audience. She was plump, dressed all in black, and had a man on each side of her—one was her husband, the other her brother.

"Who are they?" Moncharmin asked.

"My concierge," Richard replied. "This is her first time at the Opera. I gave her some good seats—she's going to be showing other people to theirs from now on, so I thought she should get to enjoy a performance first."

Moncharmin looked confused, so Richard explained that he had asked his concierge, a woman he trusted, to take over Mme. Giry's old job. He wanted to see if Box Five would still be a problem now that someone sane was in charge of it.

"Oh, by the way," said Moncharmin, "you know that Mme. Giry is planning to file a complaint against you."

"To who—the ghost?" Richard said with a laugh.

Moncharmin had nearly forgotten about the ghost altogether. The mysterious figure hadn't made a peep that night, and they were just starting to relax again when the door suddenly burst open and the stage manager rushed in, looking flustered.

"What's going on?" they both asked.

"There's a rumor," the stage manager whispered. "People say that Christine Daaé's friends are planning something against Carlotta. Carlotta's furious."

"What are you talking about?" Richard said, frowning.

But just then, the curtain rose on the fair scene, and Richard waved the stage manager away. When they were alone again, Moncharmin leaned closer to Richard and asked, "Christine has friends?"

"She does," Richard replied.

"Who?"

Richard nodded toward a nearby box where two men were seated.

"The Comte de Chagny?" Moncharmin guessed.

"Yes. He spoke to me very passionately on Christine's behalf. If I didn't know he was involved with Sorelli..."

"Really? That's interesting. And who's that pale young man sitting with him?"

"His brother. The viscount."

"He looks sick. He should be in bed."

The stage filled with music and dancing as the chorus sang cheerfully:

Red wine, white wine,

Fancy or plain,

What does it matter,

As long as there's wine?

Students, local townsfolk, soldiers, and women danced cheerfully outside the tavern, beneath a statue of Bacchus, the god of wine. Then Siebel entered the scene. Christine Daaé looked beautiful in her costume, drawing everyone's eyes. Carlotta's supporters were convinced the crowd would cheer loudly for Christine, proving that her fans were planning to stir up trouble.

But the audience stayed silent.

Then Carlotta stepped onto the stage and sang her short lines:

No, my lord, I'm no fine lady, not even a beauty,

And I don't need anyone's arm to guide my steps.

To everyone's surprise, the crowd cheered wildly. It was so over-the-top and sudden that people who hadn't heard the rumors began whispering, trying to understand what was going on.

Still, the act ended without any problems.

Everyone started saying, "Okay, it'll happen in the next act."

Some, who claimed to be in the know, whispered that the trouble would begin during The King of Thule ballad. They hurried to the subscriber entrance to warn Carlotta. Meanwhile, the managers left their box during intermission to see if they could learn more about this supposed plot. But they didn't find anything serious, and they returned shaking their heads, thinking it was all nonsense.

As soon as they entered the box, the first thing they noticed was a box of English candies sitting on the small shelf. Who had left it there?

They asked the box-keepers, but none of them had a clue. Then, right next to the candy, they spotted a pair of opera glasses. The two managers looked at each other. Neither of them felt like laughing anymore. Everything that Madame Giry had told them suddenly came back to mind... and then... they felt a strange, cold draft around them.

They sat down without a word.

The scene on stage showed Margarita's garden.

"Gentle flowers in the dew,

Carry my message to you..."

As Christine sang the first two lines, holding a bunch of roses and lilacs, she looked up and spotted the Vicomte de Chagny in his box. From that moment on, her voice didn't sound as clear and beautiful as usual. Something dulled her singing, made it feel less magical.

"She's so odd," whispered one of Carlotta's friends from the audience. "The other day she was perfect, and tonight she's just bleating. No real training."

"Gentle flowers, stay right here,

Tell her all I hold dear..."

Raoul, sitting in his box, covered his face with his hands and cried. Behind him, his older brother, the count, angrily chewed his mustache and frowned. Normally, the count was calm and composed, so for him to show his frustration like that meant he was truly furious. And he was. He had seen Raoul return from a sudden, secret trip in poor health. But when asked, Raoul gave a vague answer that didn't satisfy him. The count had written to Christine, asking to meet with her. She had the nerve to say she couldn't see him—or his brother.

"If only she would listen,

And smile to ease this pain..."

"That little schemer," the count growled.

He wondered what Christine was after. What did she want? She had a reputation for being proper. No friends. No protector. Just an innocent girl from the North... or maybe she was cleverer than she looked.

Raoul, still hiding behind his hands and wiping away tears, couldn't stop thinking about the letter he had received after returning to Paris. Christine, who had run away from Perros in the middle of the night, had arrived back before him. The letter read:

MY DEAR LITTLE PLAYFELLOW:

You have to be strong. Please don't try to see me again, or even talk about me. If you care about me at all, please do this for my sake. I will never forget you, dear Raoul. But my life depends on this. And maybe... yours does too.

YOUR LITTLE CHRISTINE

Suddenly, the Opera House erupted with applause. Carlotta had just stepped onstage.

"If only I knew who he was,

The one who spoke to me so sweetly—

Was he someone noble, or just pretending to be?"

The audience clapped loudly after she finished singing the Ballad of the King of Thule. Then again, they cheered even louder after her performance of the Jewel Song:

"Oh, what happiness beyond compare,

To wear these shining jewels so rare!"

Feeling confident in her voice and encouraged by the crowd, Carlotta gave it her all. She wasn't just performing as Margarita anymore—she transformed into a new character, bold and fiery, like Carmen. She was dramatic, passionate, and full of pride. The crowd loved it. It looked like her comeback in Faust was going to be a big win.

Until the disaster struck.

Faust was on one knee, singing:

"Let me see your face,
While the stars above
Shine softly down,
As if they're sharing in my love."

Margarita replied:
"How strange it feels—
The night wraps around me like a spell.
Its music pulls me in,
And I follow, unafraid,
Caught in its gentle magic."

But just then—right in the middle of that beautiful moment—it happened.

Carlotta made a sound. A terrible sound.

"Co-ack!" Like a giant toad.

She looked shocked. Frozen. The audience was silent, confused and stunned. In their box, the two managers gasped in horror. Everyone could feel that something wasn't right. This wasn't a normal mistake. This felt like something evil was at work.

That croak—it didn't sound human.

It was strange. It was wrong. It was terrifying.

Poor Carlotta. Humiliated. Heartbroken. Shattered.

The noise in the theater was beyond anything anyone had ever heard. If something like this had happened to anyone other than Carlotta, the crowd would've booed her off the stage. But everyone knew how perfect her voice usually was—so no one got angry. Instead, they were just shocked and horrified. It was the kind of reaction people might have if they saw a priceless statue like the Venus de Milo suddenly break apart... but even then, at least they'd understand what happened.

Here, though, the strange croak she made was impossible to explain. For a moment, even Carlotta couldn't believe it. She stood there, frozen, wondering if she'd really made that awful sound. Maybe it was her ears playing tricks on her. Maybe it wasn't her voice at all. She tried to believe it was just her imagination and not a betrayal from her own throat.

Up in Box Five, Moncharmin and Richard had turned pale. This strange, frightening moment shook them deeply—especially because, just before it happened, they had felt the ghost's presence. They could feel his breath. Moncharmin's hair stood on end. Richard wiped sweat from his forehead. The ghost was there, near them… behind them… beside them. They could feel it. They were sure there were three people in the box—but they saw only each other.

They were terrified. Frozen. They didn't dare move or speak, afraid the ghost would realize they knew he was there.

Then it happened.

"Co-ack!" The sound of their own horror escaped loudly into the theater. They felt like the ghost was attacking them now. They leaned over the edge of their box, staring at Carlotta like they didn't even recognize her. That girl—she must've been the trigger for whatever was coming. The ghost had warned them something bad would happen. The Opera House was cursed.

They sat frozen, dreading what was next. Richard could barely whisper to Carlotta, "Well, go on!"

Carlotta didn't give up. Bravely, she tried to sing the same line again—the one where her voice had failed.

The crowd went quiet. Only Carlotta's voice echoed through the hall:

"I feel without alarm..."

The audience didn't share her calm. Everyone held their breath.

"I feel without alarm... I feel without alarm—co-ack! With its melody enwind me—co-ack! And all my heart sub—co-ack!"

The croaking came back. Again and again.

Now the whole place broke into chaos. People were shouting. Screaming. The two managers sank into their chairs, too afraid to look behind them. They were sure the ghost was right there—laughing at them.

Then they heard it. A voice—impossible, terrifying—whispering right into their ears:

"She is singing tonight to bring the chandelier down!"

At once, they looked up toward the ceiling—and screamed.

The massive chandelier was falling. It had broken loose and was crashing toward the audience. It struck with a thunderous crash right in the middle of the crowd, sending people running in every direction.

The newspapers later reported many injuries—and one death.

The giant chandelier had landed on the woman who had come to the Opera for the very first time. She was the same woman Richard had chosen to replace Madame Giry as the ghost's box-keeper.

She died instantly.

The next morning, a newspaper headline read:

TWO   HUNDRED   KILOS   ON   THE   HEAD   OF   A CONCIERGE

That was all the world wrote about her. That was her only tribute.

Chapter VIII
The Mysterious Brougham

That terrible night was awful for everyone. Carlotta became sick. Christine Daaé vanished right after the performance and didn't return for two weeks. No one saw her at the Opera—or anywhere else.

Raoul was the first to notice Christine's sudden disappearance. He wrote to her at Madame Valerius's apartment, but she never replied. His worry grew every day, especially when her name no longer appeared on the Opera programs. Faust was performed without her.

One afternoon, Raoul went to the Opera managers' office to ask why Christine was missing. He found the two managers looking deeply troubled. Even their friends barely recognized them—they had lost their cheerful energy and seemed weighed down by something. They walked across the stage with their heads low, faces pale, and worry written all over them, like they were haunted or trapped by some unseen force.

The falling chandelier had caused them serious trouble. Even though the official investigation said the accident was caused by worn-out chains, both the old and new managers were supposed to have noticed the danger and fixed it. Many people noticed how distracted and nervous Richard and Moncharmin had become, and started to believe something even more terrifying than the chandelier crash was affecting them.

They were irritable with everyone—except for Madame Giry, who had been given her job back. When Raoul came to ask about Christine, they weren't friendly at all. They told him simply that she was on vacation. When he asked how long the break would last, they said coldly that it was indefinite—Christine had asked for time off because of her health.

"Then she's sick?" Raoul asked. "What's wrong with her?"

"We don't know," they said.

"Did you at least send the Opera's doctor to see her?"

"No. She didn't ask for him. And we trust her, so we took her word for it."

Raoul left the building feeling more hopeless than ever. He decided, no matter what Christine's letter had said, he had to speak to Madame Valerius. Christine had told him not to look for her again, but after everything he had witnessed—the strange events in Perros, what he heard outside her dressing room, and their conversation by the moor—he was convinced something was seriously wrong.

He believed someone was behind it all—someone dangerous. Christine's sensitive nature, her trusting heart, her childhood surrounded by legends, her deep love for her late father, and the way music seemed to take over her entire soul made her vulnerable. Especially under special, emotional moments—like what happened in the graveyard at Perros. Raoul began to wonder: who was taking advantage of her? Who was behind this?

With that question in mind, he hurried to Madame Valerius's apartment on Rue Notre-Dame-des-Victoires. His hands were shaking as he rang the bell. The maid who had once brought him into Christine's dressing room answered. He asked to speak with Madame Valerius.

"She's sick in bed and not seeing anyone," the maid told him.

"Please take her my card," Raoul said.

The maid soon came back and led him into a small, simply decorated sitting room. Portraits of Professor Valerius and old Daaé hung on the walls, facing each other.

"Madame says to please excuse her," the maid said. "She can only speak to you from her bed—she can't walk anymore."

Five minutes later, Raoul was shown into a dimly lit bedroom. In the shadows of the alcove, he could just make out Madame Valerius's kind, familiar face. Her hair had turned completely white, but her eyes still looked bright and gentle, almost like those of a child.

"M. de Chagny!" she said happily, reaching out both hands. "Ah, Heaven must've sent you! Now we can talk about HER."

That last word made Raoul's heart sink. He quickly asked,

"Madame... where is Christine?"

The old woman answered gently,

"She's with her good spirit."

"What good spirit?" Raoul cried.

"Why, the Angel of Music, of course!"

Raoul dropped into a chair. Christine was with the Angel of Music? And here was Mamma Valerius, lying in bed, smiling like it was the most natural thing in the world. She even raised a finger to her lips, signaling for him to keep quiet.

"You mustn't tell anyone," she said softly.

"You can trust me," Raoul replied.

He wasn't even sure what he was saying. His thoughts about Christine were already a mess, and now everything felt even more tangled—like the room itself was spinning, along with this sweet but strange old woman with snow-white hair and bright blue eyes.

"I know I can trust you," she said, laughing warmly. "But why are you sitting so far away? Come closer, like when you were a little boy. Give me your hands, like you used to when you brought me the story of little Lotte—Christine's story, the one her father told you. I'm very fond of you, M. Raoul. And Christine is too!"

"She's fond of me?" Raoul repeated, his heart aching. He struggled to focus—trying to make sense of the Angel of Music, of Christine's odd words, of the terrible skull-like face he had seen at the church in Perros, and of the rumors he had overheard about the Opera ghost, especially the horrible story told by Joseph Buquet before he died.

In a quiet voice, he asked, "What makes you think Christine cares about me, Madame?"

"She talked about you every day."

"Really? What did she say?"

"She said you asked her to marry you!"

The old woman laughed with pure delight.

Raoul jumped up from his chair, his face red, completely embarrassed.

"What's wrong? Where are you going? Sit down this instant!" she said. "Are you upset because I laughed? I'm sorry! But come now, this isn't your fault. You didn't know, did you? You thought Christine was free to marry?"

"Is she engaged to someone else?" Raoul asked, barely able to get the words out.

"Oh, no, no!" she said quickly. "You know Christine can't marry—even if she wanted to!"

"But I don't know anything! Why can't she?"

"Because the Angel of Music won't let her."

"I don't understand…"

"He told her she mustn't."

"He doesn't let her marry! The Angel of Music won't allow it!"

"Oh, he doesn't say it directly. But he told her that if she ever got married, she would never hear his voice again. That he would disappear forever. So you see, she can't lose him. It makes sense, doesn't it?"

"Yes, yes," Raoul said softly. "It makes sense."

"Besides," said Mme. Valerius, "I thought Christine told you all this when she saw you in Perros. She went there with her good genius."

"She went to Perros with him?" Raoul asked.

"Well, yes. He promised to meet her there, in the churchyard, at her father's grave. He said he'd play 'The Resurrection of Lazarus' on her father's violin!"

Raoul stood up suddenly, looking serious.

"Madame, please tell me where this 'genius' lives."

The old lady didn't seem bothered by the question. She looked up and answered simply, "In Heaven."

Raoul didn't know how to respond. He was completely thrown off by her honest and innocent belief that the Angel of Music came from Heaven and visited Christine backstage at the Opera.

He now started to understand how someone raised by a superstitious musician and a dreamy old lady might fall into believing something so strange. And the more he thought about it, the more worried he became.

"Christine is still... a good girl?" he asked without thinking.

"I swear it," said Mme. Valerius firmly. "And if you don't believe it, then why are you even here?"

Raoul nervously pulled at his gloves.

"How long has she known this... 'genius'?"

"About three months," she answered. "Yes, that's right. He's been giving her lessons for at least three months."

Raoul threw his hands up in frustration.

"He gives her lessons? Where?"

"Well, since she left, I don't know. But before that, he taught her in her dressing room. That wouldn't be possible in this little apartment—everyone in the building would hear. But at the Opera, at eight in the morning, no one's around. You understand now?"

"Yes," Raoul snapped. "I understand."

And with that, he rushed out, leaving Mme. Valerius wondering if the young man had lost his mind.

Raoul walked back to his brother's house, overwhelmed with emotion. He felt like punching a wall. He had believed in Christine's innocence, in her goodness! But now? The Angel of Music? He saw it clearly now—it must be some slimy tenor, some smooth-talking fake with a nice voice! How foolish he'd been!

"Oh, what a pathetic, clueless fool I've been!" he muttered angrily. "And her—how clever, how fake she must be!"

When he arrived, his older brother, the count, was waiting and welcomed him warmly. Raoul collapsed into his arms like a brokenhearted child. The count comforted him, asking no questions. Raoul didn't think he could even begin to explain the story about the Angel of Music.

Trying to lift his spirits, the count suggested they go out to dinner. Raoul was about to say no—he felt too miserable—until his brother mentioned that Christine had been seen the night before... with a man.

Raoul didn't want to believe it at first, but the details were too clear to ignore. She had been seen riding in a small carriage through the Bois de Boulogne. The window was open, and she was letting the cold air blow through. The moon was full, and she was easily recognized. The man with her stayed in the shadows, his face hidden, leaning back in the dark.

The carriage was moving slowly along a quiet path behind the Longchamp racecourse.

Raoul got dressed in a rush, hoping that going out and having fun would help him forget how upset he felt. But even at the party, he was clearly miserable. He left his brother early and, by ten o'clock that night, he was in a cab heading to the back roads near the Longchamp racecourse.

The night was freezing cold. The road was empty and lit up by the moon. Raoul told the cab driver to wait nearby, then tried to stay out of sight while stamping his feet to keep warm. He waited for about half an hour, shivering, when a quiet carriage turned the corner and came slowly toward him.

As it got closer, he saw a woman leaning out of the window. Then the moonlight hit her face just right.

"Christine!" he called out.

Her name burst from his heart before he could stop it. He wished he could take it back the second it left his mouth. The sound of her name in the quiet night seemed to trigger the driver—the carriage suddenly took off, racing past him before he could jump in front of it. The window shut quickly, and Christine's face disappeared. The carriage sped away, becoming just a shadow down the moonlit road.

"Christine!" he shouted again.

But there was no answer. He stood there, frozen and heartbroken, staring down the empty street. The night felt cold and lifeless, but not as cold and lifeless as the way he felt inside. He had thought he loved an angel, but now he believed she was just another woman who had lied to him.

Raoul, he thought, how could you let yourself be fooled like this? How could someone who seemed so innocent and sweet sneak around in the dark with a mystery man in a fancy carriage? Was all of it just an act?

She didn't even answer him.

And now, here he was, twenty years old, thinking about dying over a broken heart.

The next morning, Raoul's servant found him sitting on the edge of his bed, still in last night's clothes. He looked so pale and upset that the man feared something terrible had happened. Raoul snatched the letters from his hands, spotting Christine's handwriting right away.

The letter said:

Dear,

Please come to the Opera's masked ball the night after tomorrow. Be in the small room behind the fireplace in the main lounge at midnight. Stand near the door that leads to the Rotunda. Don't tell anyone about this meeting. Wear a white cloak and a mask. Make sure no one knows it's you.

If you love me, promise you'll do this.

Christine

Chapter IX
At the Masked Ball

The envelope was muddy and didn't have a stamp. It simply said, "To be given to M. le Vicomte Raoul de Chagny," with the address scribbled in pencil. It must've been thrown out with the hope that someone passing by would find it and deliver it, which is exactly what happened. Someone had picked it up off the sidewalk in front of the Opera House.

Raoul read it again, his eyes full of emotion. That one letter was enough to bring back all his hope. The dark picture he had imagined— Christine forgetting who she was—was quickly replaced by his original belief: she was an innocent girl caught up in something dangerous and too big for her to handle.

But just how much of a victim was she? Who was keeping her away? What kind of trap had she been pulled into? Raoul asked himself these painful questions, but even that hurt less than thinking she had lied to him. What had happened to her? Who had taken her? And how?

It had to be through music. He remembered Christine's story. After her father's death, she lost interest in everything, even singing. She went through the conservatory like a machine, with no passion. Then one day, it was like she came back to life—as if touched by something divine. She had suddenly become an amazing singer, thanks to the mysterious Angel of Music.

That same Angel had been teaching her for three months now. A very committed music teacher! And now he was taking her out for late-night drives in the Bois...

Raoul felt a deep pain in his chest. Could it really be that Christine had been toying with him this whole time? Could an opera singer fool someone as naive as him so easily? He didn't know what to think anymore. One moment he pitied her, the next he was angry. In the end, he decided to go to the masquerade ball and bought a white cloak and mask.

The night finally came. Dressed in a white costume and mask with lace around the edges, Raoul thought he looked silly—like a clown. Men of high society didn't usually go to balls like this in costume. But at least, he thought, no one would recognize him.

This ball was different from the usual. It was thrown in honor of a well-known artist and was expected to be louder, wilder, and more colorful than normal. Artists and their students flooded the place, laughing and shouting as the night went on.

Raoul hurried up the Opera's grand staircase just before midnight. He didn't stop to admire the costumes or respond to any jokes or teasing from the guests. He even got caught in a spinning crowd of dancers but managed to break free and reach the little room Christine mentioned in her letter.

The room was packed. People going to get champagne bumped into those returning from supper. The energy was chaotic. Raoul leaned against a doorframe and waited.

He didn't have to wait long. A person in a black cloak walked past and quickly squeezed his fingertips. He knew it was her. He followed without saying a word.

"Christine?" he whispered, trying not to be overheard.

The black figure turned and pressed a finger to her lips, telling him to stay quiet. He kept following her.

Raoul was scared she might vanish again. But now, he didn't feel angry anymore. He was sure Christine hadn't done anything wrong. However strange her behavior seemed, she had a reason, and he was ready to forgive her—no matter what. He loved her.

And he hoped she was finally going to explain everything.

As Raoul followed the black domino through the busy main hall again, he noticed a crowd gathered around someone whose costume was causing quite a stir. The person was dressed completely in red, with a huge hat decorated with feathers and a creepy skull mask. A long red velvet cape dragged behind him like a royal train. Embroidered in gold letters on the cape were the words: "Don't touch me! I am Red Death walking among you!"

One man got bold and tried to touch him—instantly, a skeleton hand shot out from the red sleeve and grabbed the man's wrist. The touch was so cold and strong, the man screamed in fear and pain. When Red Death let go, the man ran off in terror while the onlookers laughed.

Just then, Raoul passed in front of this eerie figure, who had turned his way. Raoul nearly shouted, "The skull face from Perros-Guirec!" He recognized him! He wanted to run after him, forgetting Christine, but the black domino—clearly alarmed—grabbed his arm and pulled him away from the crowd. She looked over her shoulder a couple of times, clearly seeing something that worried her, and hurried even faster.

They climbed two floors. By then, the halls and stairways were nearly empty. The black domino opened the door to a private box and motioned for Raoul to follow. Once inside, she closed the door behind them and whispered for him to stay in the back and not let anyone see him. Raoul took off his mask. Christine kept hers on. When he was about to ask her to take it off, she pressed her ear to the wall and listened. Then she cracked open the door, peeking out.

"He must've gone higher," she whispered. Suddenly, she said, "Wait—he's coming back down!"

She tried to shut the door quickly, but Raoul stopped her. On the top step, he had seen a red shoe—then another—and then the entire red costume of the Red Death. And once again, he saw the terrible skull mask from the graveyard in Perros.

"It's him!" Raoul said. "This time, he won't get away—"

But Christine slammed the door just before Raoul could run out. He tried to push past her.

"Who do you mean?" she asked, her voice suddenly tense. "Who won't get away?"

Raoul tried to shove her aside, but she blocked him with surprising strength. His anger exploded.

"Who? The man behind that awful skull mask! The one from the churchyard at Perros! Red Death! Your so-called friend—the Angel of Music! But I'm going to rip off his mask, and this time, we'll face each other, no more lies! I'll see who you really love!"

He let out a bitter laugh while Christine let out a sad sound behind her mask. She stretched out her arms to block the door.

"For the sake of our love, Raoul—you can't go out there!"

He froze. What had she just said? "Our love"? She had never said that before. Was she saying it just to stall him?

He didn't believe it. In a voice full of hurt, he said:

"You're lying! You don't love me—you never did! What a fool I was to believe you! Why did you give me hope at Perros—real hope—when all along you were playing me? You've tricked everyone, even poor Madame Valerius, who still thinks you're an innocent girl! And now here you are, running around the Opera Ball with Red Death! I'm ashamed of you!"

Tears filled his eyes. Christine didn't stop him. She had only one goal: to keep him from leaving the box.

"One day, Raoul," she said softly, "you'll regret saying these things, and when you ask for forgiveness—I'll give it."

Raoul shook his head. "No. You've made me crazy. I can't believe I ever wanted to marry someone like you—an Opera girl!"

"Raoul... how can you say that?"

Christine's voice sounded serious and different as she said, "No, my dear, live! And... goodbye. Goodbye, Raoul..."

Raoul stepped forward unsteadily, trying to hide his pain with sarcasm: "Oh, so I can come and cheer for you now and then?"

"I will never sing again, Raoul," she replied.

"Really?" he responded with more sarcasm. "So, he's taking you off the stage? Congratulations! But maybe we'll run into each other in the park one evening."

"Not in the park or anywhere else, Raoul. You won't see me again."

"Can I at least ask what darkness you're going back to? What kind of hell are you heading for, mysterious lady... or is it heaven?"

"I came to tell you, dear, but I can't now... you wouldn't believe me! You've lost trust in me, Raoul; it's over!"

Her despairing tone made Raoul feel guilty for his harshness.

"But listen!" he pleaded. "Can't you explain all this? You're free; no one is stopping you. You move around Paris, you wore a disguise to come to the ball... why not just go home? What have you been doing these past two weeks? What's this story about the Angel of Music you've been telling Mamma Valerius? Maybe someone has tricked you, taken advantage of your innocence. I saw something myself at Perros... but surely you know the truth now! You seem sensible, Christine. You know what you're doing... Meanwhile, Mamma Valerius is waiting for you at home, calling for your 'good genius!' Please, Christine, explain! Anyone could have been fooled like I was. What's going on?"

Christine removed her mask and said, "Dear, it's a tragedy."

Seeing her face, Raoul couldn't hide his shock and fear. The healthy glow she once had was gone. Her face was pale, with deep lines of sorrow and dark shadows under her eyes.

"My love! My love!" he cried, reaching out to her. "You promised to forgive me..."

"Maybe... someday, maybe," she said, putting her mask back on. She turned to leave, signaling him not to follow.

He wanted to go after her, but she turned back and firmly gestured goodbye, making him stay put.

He watched her until she disappeared. Then he wandered through the crowd, his mind in turmoil, his heart aching. As he crossed the dance floor, he asked if anyone had seen the Red Death. Yes, everyone had seen him; but Raoul couldn't find him. By two in the morning, he was walking down the hallway behind the stage, heading toward Christine Daaé's dressing room.

His steps led him to the room where his heart had first been broken. He knocked on the door. No answer. He entered, just like when he had searched for "the man's voice." The room was empty. A dim light burned from a gas lamp. He noticed some paper on a small desk. Thinking of writing to Christine, he suddenly heard footsteps in the hallway. He quickly hid in the inner room, separated from the dressing room by a curtain.

Christine entered, removed her mask with a tired motion, and tossed it onto the table. She sighed and rested her head in her hands. What was she thinking about? Raoul? No, because he heard her whisper, "Poor Erik!"

At first, he thought he misheard. He believed that if anyone deserved pity, it was him, Raoul. It would have made sense if she had said, "Poor Raoul," after what had happened between them. But she shook her head and repeated, "Poor Erik!"

What did this Erik have to do with Christine's sighs? Why was she feeling sorry for Erik when Raoul was so unhappy?

Christine began writing calmly and deliberately, filling several pages. Suddenly, she stopped, hid the papers in her dress, and seemed to listen intently. Raoul listened too. Where was that strange sound coming from? A faint singing seemed to come from the walls... yes, it was as if the walls themselves were singing! The song grew clearer; the words became distinguishable. He heard a voice—a very beautiful, soft, captivating voice—but it was definitely a man's voice. The voice came closer and closer, through the wall, approaching... and now the voice was in the room, right in front of Christine. She stood up and spoke to the voice as if addressing someone:

"Here I am, Erik," she said. "I'm ready. But you're late."

Raoul, peeking from behind the curtain, couldn't believe his eyes—he saw nothing. Christine's face brightened. A smile of happiness appeared on her pale lips, a smile like that of someone who finally feels hope after a long illness.

The bodiless voice kept singing. Raoul had never heard anything so deeply beautiful, haunting, and powerful all at once. It was soft yet strong, sweet yet commanding—completely impossible to resist. As he listened, almost trembling, he finally began to understand how Christine Daaé could step onto the stage one night and stun everyone with a voice so beautiful it felt otherworldly—still under the spell of this invisible teacher.

The voice was performing the Wedding-night Song from Romeo and Juliet. Raoul watched as Christine reached her arms toward the voice, just like she had in the churchyard at Perros when the unseen violin played The Resurrection of Lazarus. The voice poured emotion into the line:

"Destiny has tied us together, now and always!"

The words cut through Raoul's heart. He struggled to resist the spell this voice seemed to cast over everything—draining his strength, his will, even his sense of reality—at the very moment he needed them most. Somehow, he found the courage to pull aside the curtain hiding him, and he stepped forward.

Christine was walking toward the back of the room, where a giant mirror covered the wall. Her reflection stared back at her—but Raoul, standing just behind her, cast no reflection at all, hidden entirely by her figure.

"Destiny has tied us together, now and always!"

Christine reached toward the mirror, and her reflection did the same. Slowly, the real Christine and the image moved closer until they touched. Raoul reached out his arms, hoping to catch them both in one embrace.

But suddenly, a strange light flashed, and he was knocked backward as a cold gust hit his face. Around him, Christines spun in circles—two, four, eight, maybe twenty versions of her, all laughing and dancing just out of reach. He tried to grab one, but they vanished as quickly as they had appeared. When everything calmed, all that remained in the mirror was his own reflection.

Christine was gone.

He rushed to the mirror, pounding on the glass and walls. Nothing. No sign of her. And all the while, that same voice kept singing from somewhere far away:

"Destiny has tied us together, now and always!"

Where had she gone? Would she come back?

But hadn't she told him it was over between them? And didn't the voice just keep repeating—

"Destiny has tied us together, now and always!"

To me? Who was me?

Exhausted, defeated, and lost in confusion, Raoul dropped into the chair Christine had been sitting in. Like her, he lowered his head into his hands. When he finally looked up, his face was wet with heavy tears—the kind only true heartbreak can bring. Tears that fall when love feels real and deeply painful.

And softly, to no one in particular, he whispered:

"Who is this Erik?"

Chapter X
Forget the Name of the Man's Voice

The day after Christine disappeared in that strange flash of light, Raoul went to visit Mamma Valerius to see if she had come back. When he arrived, he found a peaceful scene—Christine was sitting beside the old woman's bed, who was sitting up and knitting. Christine looked much healthier than before. Her cheeks were rosy again, and the tired look in her eyes was gone. Raoul could hardly believe she was the same person he'd seen just the day before. If it weren't for the tiny hint of sadness still in her eyes, he might have thought he imagined everything.

Christine stood up and calmly offered Raoul her hand, without showing any emotion. Raoul was so shocked, he couldn't move or speak.

"Well, M. de Chagny," Mamma Valerius said cheerfully, "don't you recognize Christine? Her good angel brought her back to us!"

"Mamma!" Christine said quickly, her cheeks turning red. "I thought we agreed not to talk about that anymore. You know there's no such thing as the Angel of Music."

"But he gave you lessons for three months!"

"Mamma, I promised I would explain everything to you one day—and I will. But until then, you promised not to ask questions."

"I only agreed because you promised you'd never leave me again. Did you keep that promise, Christine?"

"Mamma, this has nothing to do with M. de Chagny."

"It actually does," Raoul said, trying to stay steady even though his voice was shaky. "Everything about you matters to me. I'm surprised but happy to see you here after what happened yesterday. After what you said—and what I guessed—I didn't expect to see you so soon. I would be thrilled that you're back if you weren't hiding something. Christine, this could be dangerous. I've known you too long not to be worried. If you don't let someone help you, something bad could happen."

At that, Mamma Valerius sat up quickly, clearly upset.

"What are you saying? Christine is in danger?"

"Yes, madame," Raoul answered, even as Christine silently begged him to stop.

"Oh no!" the old woman cried. "Christine, you have to tell me what's going on! Why did you hide this from me? What kind of danger, M. de Chagny?"

"Someone is tricking her," Raoul said.

"You mean the Angel of Music?" Mamma Valerius asked.

"She already told you he's not real."

"Then what is this? Oh, I can't take this stress!"

"There's something serious going on," Raoul said. "It's more terrifying than ghosts or fairy tales. And it's affecting all of us—Christine, you, and me."

Mamma Valerius looked at Christine in fear. Christine rushed to her and hugged her tightly.

"Don't listen to him, Mamma. Please don't believe him," she whispered.

"Then promise me you'll never leave me again," the old woman begged.

Christine didn't answer.

"That's the promise you need to make," Raoul said. "That's the only way to protect her and give you peace, madame. We won't ask any questions about the past. Just promise you'll stay safe."

"I never asked you to protect me," Christine said firmly. "And I won't make that promise. I decide what to do with my life, M. de Chagny. You don't have any right to control me. And about where I've been these past two weeks—only one person has the right to ask me that: my husband. But I don't have a husband, and I don't plan to marry."

She lifted her hands as if to end the discussion. But then Raoul noticed something that made his heart stop—a plain gold ring on her finger.

"You say you're not married," he said, "but you're wearing a wedding ring."

He reached out to take her hand, but she quickly pulled it away.

"It's just a gift!" she said, blushing and clearly nervous.

"Christine! If you're not married, then someone gave you that ring because they want to marry you. Why are you still hiding the truth? Why keep hurting me like this? That ring is a promise—and you clearly said yes to it."

"That's what I thought too!" Mamma Valerius said. "And what did she say when you asked her?"

"What I chose," Christine snapped, clearly frustrated. "Don't you think this questioning has gone on long enough, monsieur? As far as I'm concerned—"

Raoul quickly interrupted her before she could finish.

"I'm sorry for how I spoke to you, Christine. I know I'm getting involved in things you probably believe aren't my business. But please, let me tell you what I saw—and I saw more than you might think. Or at least, I think I saw it. Honestly, it was so strange I've started to question if I imagined it."

Christine looked at him, her expression tight. "Then tell me—what do you think you saw?"

"I saw your face light up when you heard that voice," Raoul said quietly. "That voice coming through the wall or the room next to yours... I saw the joy on your face, Christine. And that's what has me so worried. You're under a dangerous spell. And what's strange is, you admitted today there's no Angel of Music. So if that's true, Christine, why did you follow him? Why did you look so radiant, like you were truly hearing something divine? That voice is dangerous, Christine. I know, because it affected me too. I was so mesmerized that I didn't even see where you went. You disappeared right in front of me!

"Christine... in the name of Heaven, in the name of your father, who loved you and who also loved me like a son—please, tell us who that voice belongs to. If you tell us, we can help you. Just say the name. Tell us the name of the man who dared to put a ring on your finger."

"M. de Chagny," Christine said coldly, "you'll never know."

Hearing Christine speak so sharply, Mamma Valerius suddenly took her side.

"And even if she does love this man," the old woman said firmly, "that's none of your business, monsieur!"

"Maybe not," Raoul replied, his voice soft, tears rising in his eyes, "but I believe Christine does love him. And what truly breaks my heart is that I'm not even sure this man is worthy of her love."

"That's for me to decide," Christine said, glaring at Raoul.

"When a man tries to win a girl's love with tricks and secrecy like this—"

"That means he's either a villain or the girl is a fool? Is that what you're saying?"

"Christine!"

"Raoul, how can you judge someone you've never seen? Someone no one really knows—someone you know nothing about!"

"I do know one thing, Christine… I know his name. The name you never meant for me to find out. The name of your 'Angel of Music'… is Erik!"

Christine gasped, going pale. "Who told you that?"

"You did."

"What do you mean?"

"The night of the masked ball… when you went back to your dressing room, I heard you whisper, 'Poor Erik.' And there was a poor Raoul who heard you."

"This is the second time you've spied on me, M. de Chagny!"

"I wasn't spying outside the door. I was already inside… in the little room behind your dressing room."

Christine let out a cry of fear. Her face filled with panic.

"Oh no… you poor, foolish man! Do you want to die?"

"Maybe," Raoul said softly.

There was so much pain and love in his voice that Christine's anger melted away. She took his hands, tears in her eyes, and looked at him with a tenderness that showed just how much she cared.

"Raoul," she said, "forget about the voice. Forget his name. Promise me you'll never try to uncover the truth behind it."

"Is it really that dangerous?" he asked.

"It's the most terrifying secret in the world," she whispered. "Swear you'll never try to find out. Swear you'll never go to my dressing room unless I ask you to."

"Then promise me you'll ask for me sometimes," he said gently.

"I promise."

"When?"

"Tomorrow."

"Then I swear to do what you ask."

He kissed her hands and left, his heart torn. As he walked away, he silently cursed Erik—but told himself to be patient.

Chapter XI
Above the Trap-Doors

The next day, Raoul saw Christine again at the Opera. She was still wearing the simple gold ring on her finger. She acted sweet and gentle, and they talked about his future—his plans, his career, and what was coming next.

Raoul told her the date for the Polar expedition had been moved up, and that he'd be leaving France in three weeks, maybe even sooner. Christine smiled and told him he should be excited—it was a step toward becoming famous. But when Raoul told her that fame meant nothing to him without love, she acted like he was just being dramatic and childish.

"How can you joke about something so serious?" he asked. "What if we never see each other again? I could die on that trip."

"Or I could," Christine said softly.

This time she wasn't smiling. She looked serious, like she had just realized something. Her eyes were lit up, not with joy, but with something deeper.

"What are you thinking, Christine?" Raoul asked.

"I'm thinking we'll never see each other again," she replied.

"And that makes you look happy?" he asked, confused.

"I'm thinking that in a month, we'll have to say goodbye forever."

"Unless," Raoul said, "we make a promise to wait for each other— to stay true."

Christine quickly put her hand over his mouth.

"No, Raoul," she said. "We both know we can't do that. We're not getting married. That's final."

But then, all of a sudden, she brightened up. She clapped her hands like an excited child and smiled. Raoul looked at her in shock.

"But," she said, holding out both her hands to him like a gift, "if we can't get married, we can at least be secretly engaged. Just for one month. No one will know—just us. People have had secret weddings before, so why not a secret engagement? We'll belong to each other for this one month. Then you'll leave, and I'll always have the memory of that month."

She looked so happy with the idea. Then her face turned serious again.

"This way, we can have something beautiful... and no one will be hurt."

Raoul loved the idea. He playfully bowed and said, "Mademoiselle, may I have the honor of your hand?"

Christine laughed. "You already have both of them, my dear fiancé! Oh, Raoul, we're going to be so happy. Let's pretend to be engaged all day, every day!"

They treated it like a game—the most wonderful game. They made up sweet speeches and promises to each other, pretending to be a real couple. But it wasn't just pretend. They were giving each other their hearts, and they had to be very careful not to break them.

About a week into their "game," things started to go wrong. Raoul got too serious, too emotional. His heart felt crushed, and he suddenly said:

"I'm not going to the North Pole!"

Christine, who hadn't even considered he might feel that way, realized their pretend game had become real—and maybe dangerous. She felt guilty. She didn't say a word. She just quietly left and went home.

That afternoon, they'd been in her dressing room, like they were every day. Their simple little dates included three biscuits, two glasses of port, and a small bunch of violets. But that night, Christine didn't perform, and Raoul didn't get her usual letter, even though they'd promised to write to each other daily for a month.

The next morning, worried and confused, Raoul rushed to see Mamma Valerius. Calmly, she told him Christine had left the day before at five o'clock and would be gone for two days.

Raoul was crushed. He couldn't believe Mamma Valerius could share something so upsetting without showing any concern. He tried asking more questions, but it was clear she didn't know anything else.

Christine came back the next day—and it felt like a big victory. She repeated her amazing performance from the gala night. Ever since the "toad" incident, Carlotta hadn't dared return to the stage. Just the thought of croaking like that again filled her with fear and made it impossible for her to sing. She was so embarrassed by what had happened that she ended her contract. Christine was offered her spot, at least for the time being, and she was met with huge applause during La Juive.

Raoul, who of course was in the audience, was the only one not celebrating. Christine was still wearing the simple gold ring—and it hadn't come from him. A quiet voice in his mind whispered, "She's wearing the ring again tonight. But you didn't give it to her. She gave her heart tonight... and it wasn't to you. If she won't tell you where she's been these last two days... you'll have to ask Erik."

He rushed backstage and waited where she'd see him. When Christine spotted him—because she had clearly been looking—she said quickly, "Come with me!" and pulled him toward her dressing room.

Raoul dropped to his knees in front of her. He promised he would leave on the expedition if she would promise never to hide their happiness again. Christine cried and they kissed like a pair of grieving siblings—like two people brought together by loss and pain.

Then, all of a sudden, she pulled away. She seemed to hear something. She pointed quickly to the door. As he stepped through, she whispered so softly he could barely make it out, "Tomorrow, my dear fiancé! Be happy, Raoul—I sang for you tonight!"

Raoul returned the next day, but something had changed. Their short time apart had broken the magic of their pretend engagement. Sitting together in her dressing room, they looked at each other with sad eyes and said nothing. Raoul had to fight the urge to shout, "I'm jealous! I'm jealous!" But even without speaking, Christine seemed to hear it.

"Let's take a walk," she said gently. "Some fresh air will help."

Raoul thought she meant a walk far away from the Opera—the building he now hated, which felt like a prison watched over by Erik. But instead, she led him to the stage and had him sit on the edge of a stage well, surrounded by props set for the evening show.

Another time, they wandered hand in hand through an empty indoor garden. Everything was fake—cut-out vines, painted flowers, a ceiling painted like the sky. It was like Christine wasn't allowed to see or feel the real world anymore. The only "air" she could breathe came from the theater. A fireman sometimes passed by, quietly keeping an eye on them as they walked in silence.

She would lead him up above the stage, high into the rafters, where ropes and beams crisscrossed like a tangled forest. She loved running ahead of him across the shaky catwalks, laughing as he followed nervously.

"If you were really a sailor," she'd tease, "you wouldn't be afraid!"

Then they'd return "to earth"—which meant a back hallway that took them to the ballet school. There, little girls no older than six practiced their steps, dreaming of someday being famous ballerinas dripping in diamonds. In the meantime, Christine gave them candy.

She showed Raoul around the costume and prop rooms, proudly guiding him through her whole world. It wasn't real, but it was massive—seventeen stories tall from the basement to the roof. Hundreds of people worked there. Christine was like a beloved queen, known and loved by all. She'd stop to chat with the workers, sit with them as they worked, and offer helpful advice as they cut fabric or polished jewelry for the next show.

There were shoemakers, goldsmiths, and many other craftsmen. Christine knew all of them, cared about their worries, and listened to their stories.

She even introduced Raoul to the hidden corners of the Opera, where old retired couples lived quietly and had long been forgotten. She'd knock on their doors and say, "This is my Prince Charming." Then they'd sit on old theater props and listen to stories—legends of the Opera, like fairy tales. These old people had lived in the Opera for so long that they'd forgotten the world outside. Kings and governments had come and gone, but they were still there, untouched by time.

The days passed quickly, and Christine and Raoul tried to act like everything was normal. They filled their time with small adventures and talked about other things, pretending not to think about what was really on their minds. But one thing was clear—Christine, who had always seemed stronger than Raoul, was now more nervous than ever.

During their walks, she would suddenly start running for no reason, then stop just as quickly. Her hand would go cold and grip his tightly, as if afraid. Sometimes her eyes seemed to follow something that wasn't really there. She would call out, "This way! This way!" laughing in a breathless, shaky way that sometimes ended in tears. When Raoul tried to ask what was wrong—even before he finished the question— she would answer in a rushed voice, "It's nothing. I swear, it's nothing."

One day, as they walked across the stage, they passed by an open trapdoor leading into darkness below. Raoul stopped and looked down.

"You've shown me everything above the stage," he said, "but I've heard strange stories about what's below. Can we go down there?"

Christine grabbed him tightly, like she was afraid he'd fall in. Her voice trembled as she whispered, "Never! I won't let you go down there. That place doesn't belong to me. Everything underground belongs to him."

Raoul looked her in the eyes. "So, he lives down there?"

"I never said that!" she snapped. "Who told you such a thing? Let's go. Sometimes I wonder if you've lost your mind, Raoul. You take everything too far. Come on, now!"

She tried to pull him away, but Raoul resisted. He wanted to stay by the trapdoor. Something about that dark hole drew him in. But suddenly, the trapdoor slammed shut—so fast neither of them saw who closed it. They were both left stunned.

"Maybe he was there," Raoul said quietly.

Christine tried to brush it off, but she looked uneasy.

"No, no... it was just the stage crew. They open and close those doors for no real reason—it's just their job. Same with the other doors around here. They're always keeping busy."

"But what if it was him?" Raoul asked.

"No! He's locked himself away. He's working."

"Working? Really?" Raoul said, clearly not convinced.

"Yes. He can't mess with trapdoors and work at the same time," she said, shivering.

"What's he working on?" Raoul asked.

"Something awful," she said. "But that's good for us. When he works like that, he doesn't eat, sleep, or notice anything. He becomes like a ghost—he forgets we even exist." She shivered again and held Raoul tightly.

Then she said quietly, "But what if it really was him?"

"Are you afraid of him?" Raoul asked.

"No, of course not," she said quickly—but her behavior said otherwise.

Over the next few days, Christine avoided going near the trapdoors. Her nervousness kept getting worse. Finally, one afternoon, she showed up late. Her face was pale, and her eyes were red like she'd been crying. Raoul decided he couldn't take it anymore. He was ready to do whatever it took—even if it meant giving up his Polar expedition—if she didn't tell him the truth about the voice.

"Stop! Don't say that out loud!" Christine said in a panic, her eyes darting around the room. "What if he heard you, Raoul?"

"I'm going to get you away from him, Christine," Raoul said. "You'll be free of him. I promise. You won't even think about him anymore."

"Do you really think that's possible?" she asked softly.

That small bit of doubt in her voice gave Raoul hope. He took her up to the highest floor of the Opera House—far away from the trapdoors.

"I'll hide you somewhere in the world where he can't find you," he said. "You'll be safe. And since you've sworn never to marry, I'll disappear after that."

Christine squeezed his hands tightly, filled with emotion. But then, as if afraid again, she turned her head and said, "Higher... we need to go higher."

She pulled him upward through the maze of wooden beams and supports above the stage. They climbed through rafters, stepping from beam to beam like they were running through a forest made of wood and ropes.

Christine kept looking behind her nervously, but she didn't notice the shadow that followed her step for step. It stopped when she stopped. It moved when she moved. It didn't make a sound. Raoul didn't see it either—because as long as he could see Christine, nothing else mattered.

Chapter XII
Apollo's Lyre

They made their way up to the roof. Christine moved across it lightly, like a bird. Together, they looked out over the space between the domes and the large triangular part of the building. She breathed deeply, feeling free as she looked out over all of Paris below, busy and full of life. She called Raoul to her side, and they walked together along the narrow metal paths and wide lead walkways. They saw their reflections in huge water tanks—filled with still water—where, during hot weather, the young ballet boys practiced swimming and diving.

A shadow followed close behind them, quietly and without being noticed. The couple had no idea it was there as they sat down, feeling safe under the great statue of Apollo, who raised his bronze lyre toward a sky glowing red with the sunset.

It was a beautiful spring evening. Wisps of clouds, lit with gold and purple from the setting sun, drifted slowly overhead. Christine turned to Raoul and said:

"Soon, we'll travel farther and faster than those clouds—maybe even to the ends of the earth. And then you'll leave me. But if, when the time comes, I say I can't go with you... then you'll have to take me by force."

"Are you afraid you'll change your mind, Christine?" Raoul asked.

"I don't know," she said, shaking her head in a strange way. "He's like a demon." She shivered and curled into his arms. "I'm scared of going back down to him... underground."

"Then why go back at all?" he asked.

"If I don't, something terrible might happen! But I don't think I can do it, Raoul... I know we're supposed to feel sorry for someone who lives hidden underground... but he's terrifying! And the time is almost here—I only have one day left. If I don't go, he'll come get me with his voice. He'll drag me back down... and he'll kneel in front of me with that skull-like face and tell me he loves me! He'll cry, Raoul—cry with black, empty eyes. I can't bear to see that again!"

She broke down in tears, and Raoul held her close.

"No, Christine. You'll never have to hear him say he loves you again. You won't see those tears! Let's run away. Right now!"

He tried to pull her to her feet, but she stopped him.

"No, not yet," she said sadly. "It would be too cruel... let him hear me sing tomorrow night. Then we'll leave. Come to my dressing room at midnight. He'll be waiting for me in the dining room by the lake... that will be our chance. We'll escape, and you must promise to take me, even if I say no—because if I go back this time, I might never return."

As she sighed, she thought she heard another sigh behind her.

"Did you hear that?" she asked.

Her teeth were chattering.

"No," Raoul said. "I didn't hear anything."

"This is horrible," Christine whispered. "Always being afraid like this! And yet, we're safe up here. We're in the open air, under the sun. He can't stand sunlight. I've never seen him in daylight... it must be awful. The first time I saw him, I thought he was going to die."

"Why?" Raoul asked, now very uneasy.

"Because I had seen him."

Raoul and Christine both turned at once.

"I thought I heard someone," Raoul said. "Maybe someone's hurt. Did you hear it?"

"I'm not sure," Christine said. "Even when he's not near, I still hear his sighs. But if you heard something too…"

They got up and looked around. But they were completely alone on the wide metal roof. They sat down again, and Raoul asked softly:

"Tell me how you first saw him."

"I heard him for three months before I ever saw him," she said. "At first, like you, I thought his beautiful voice was just coming from the next room. I left my dressing room and looked everywhere. But, as you know, my room is very isolated, and the voice wasn't outside—it was coming from inside. And it didn't just sing; it spoke to me. It answered my questions like a real person. But the voice was so perfect—like an angel's."

Christine paused, then continued, "My father had promised me the Angel of Music would visit me after he died. I really think Mamma Valerius helped me believe. When I told her about the voice, she said, 'It must be the Angel! Go ahead and talk to him.' So I did. And the voice told me it was the Angel—the one my father had promised."

"After that, we became great friends. He asked if he could give me singing lessons every day. I agreed, and I never missed one. We always met in my dressing room. But you can't imagine what those lessons were like."

"No," Raoul said. "What did you use for music?"

The music that played during my lessons was unlike anything I'd ever heard. It came from behind the wall, perfectly timed, as if it knew exactly what notes I needed. The voice seemed to understand me completely—like it knew exactly where my father had left off when he taught me to sing. Within just a few weeks, I barely recognized my own voice. I was even scared by how much I had changed. It felt like something magical—or even unnatural—was behind it. But Mamma Valerius comforted me, saying I was too innocent to be tricked by anything evil.

The voice told me to keep our secret, so only it, Mamma Valerius, and I knew what was going on. Strangely, when I sang outside of my dressing room, my voice sounded normal again, and no one noticed anything different. I did everything the voice told me. It said, "Just wait and see—we'll amaze all of Paris!" So I waited, and lived in a kind of dreamy happiness.

That was when I saw you for the first time, Raoul. I was so happy to see you that I didn't hide my joy when I got back to my room. But the voice was already there, and it noticed something was different. It asked what had happened, and I told it everything—I didn't think there was any reason to hide the truth or keep your place in my heart a secret. After that, the voice went completely silent. I called out, begged it to answer, but it said nothing. I was so scared it might be gone forever. Oh, Raoul, how I wish it had been.

That night, I went home feeling miserable. I told Mamma Valerius, and she said, "Of course the voice is jealous!" That's when I realized... I loved you.

Christine stopped and rested her head on Raoul's shoulder. They sat like that in silence, unaware that nearby, two dark wings were moving silently across the roof—so close they could have wrapped around the couple and hidden them from sight.

"The next day," Christine went on with a sigh, "I returned to my dressing room, lost in thought. The voice came back. It sounded so sad. It told me that if I was going to give my heart to someone on earth, then it would leave me and go back to Heaven. It spoke with such deep sorrow that I should have realized something was wrong, that maybe it wasn't really an angel after all. But I couldn't let go. I still believed it was the spirit my father had promised to send. My greatest fear was losing it forever.

"I thought about my feelings for you, Raoul. I realized it was dangerous to fall in love—and I wasn't even sure if you remembered me. Besides, you were from a noble family, and I could never dream of marrying you. So I swore to the voice that you were nothing more than a friend, like a brother, and that my heart was incapable of love. That's why I ignored you when we met on stage or in the halls.

"But in our lessons, the voice lifted me into another world. Eventually, it told me, 'Now, Christine Daaé, you can give the world a little piece of Heaven's music.' I don't know why Carlotta didn't show up at the theater that night or why I was asked to take her place. But I sang like I never had before—it felt like my soul had left my body."

"Oh, Christine," Raoul said. "I could feel every emotion in your voice that night. I saw the tears on your face and cried with you. How could you sing like that while crying?"

"I was close to fainting," Christine replied. "I closed my eyes. When I opened them, you were there. But so was the voice, Raoul! I was afraid for you. That's why I pretended not to know you and laughed when you mentioned finding my scarf in the sea. But I couldn't hide it from the voice—it recognized you, and it was jealous. It said that if I didn't love you, I wouldn't avoid you, I'd treat you like any other old friend. It got angry and kept accusing me.

"At last, I said, 'That's enough! I'm going to Perros tomorrow to visit my father's grave, and I'm asking Raoul de Chagny to come with me.' The voice replied, 'Do as you please. But I will be in Perros too, because I am always where you are. And if you are still worthy of me— if you haven't lied to me—I will play "The Resurrection of Lazarus" at midnight on your father's grave, using your father's own violin.'

"That's why I wrote to you. That's how I lured you to Perros. How could I have been so fooled? Why didn't I realize the voice was just a man, not some angel? But by then, Raoul... I wasn't myself anymore. I belonged to him."

"But, Christine," Raoul cried, "you did learn the truth eventually. Why didn't you break free then? Why stay trapped in that awful nightmare?"

Christine shook her head. "Oh, Raoul. I didn't fall into the nightmare until I learned the truth. Please, pity me. You remember that awful night? When Carlotta lost her voice on stage, and the chandelier crashed down, killing and hurting people? Everyone screamed in terror. My first thoughts were of you—and of the voice. I had seen you in your brother's box and knew you were safe. But the voice had said it would be there, so I worried it might have been hurt too.

"I was still on stage and almost ran into the audience to look for it among the victims. Then I thought, 'If it's alive, it will be in my dressing room.' So I ran there. But it wasn't there either. I locked the door and begged it, through my tears, to show itself if it was still alive.

"Then I heard it—that long, sorrowful melody I knew so well. It was the same we heard at Perros, Raoul. The music of Lazarus coming back to life. And then the voice sang, 'Come! Believe in me! Whoever believes in me shall live... shall never die!' The music had such power over me. It was like a command just for me. I felt myself moving toward it without thinking. The voice pulled me in. I followed.

"My dressing room seemed to stretch longer and longer—like a hallway with no end. I know now it must have been mirrors... I had been standing in front of the mirror. But somehow, without realizing it, I had stepped through and was no longer in the room."

"What? You were outside your room and don't even know how you got there? Christine, you've got to stop dreaming!"

"I wasn't dreaming," Christine said softly. "I really found myself outside my room, without any idea how I got there. You saw me disappear once, Raoul—maybe you can explain it. But I can't. One moment I was in front of my mirror, and the next, it was gone. My whole dressing room was gone. I was standing in a dark hallway. I got scared and started to cry out. Everything was silent, except for a faint red glow in a far corner. The singing had stopped, the violin too. I called out again, and that's when something touched my hand... not a normal hand, but something cold and bony that grabbed my wrist and wouldn't let go. I screamed again. Then an arm went around my waist and held me up. I struggled for a second, but then I couldn't fight anymore. I was pulled toward the red light. That's when I realized a man was holding me—he was wearing a long cloak and a mask that covered his whole face.

"I tried to scream again, but his hand covered my mouth. I'll never forget how it felt... like death. I fainted.

"When I woke up, it was still dark. A lantern was glowing on the ground near a bubbling well. Water splashed from it and disappeared through the floor. I was lying on the ground, my head resting on the man's knee. He was soaking my forehead, and again his hands smelled like death. I tried to push him away and asked, 'Who are you? Where's the voice?' But he didn't answer—he just sighed.

"Then I felt warm air near my face and saw something white beside him in the shadows. He picked me up and placed me on it. That's when I heard a soft neigh. I whispered, 'César!' It was the white horse from The Prophet! I had fed him sugar and treats so many times. I remembered how people once said the Opera Ghost had stolen the horse. I believed in the voice, but I never believed in the ghost—until that moment. Now I wasn't so sure. I was afraid. I wondered if the ghost had taken me prisoner. I called out for the voice, begging it to help me... because I still didn't think they were the same person.

"You've heard of the Opera Ghost, haven't you, Raoul?"

"Yes," Raoul said. "But what happened next, when you were on the horse?"

"I didn't try to move. I let him hold me. The strangest feeling came over me—it was peaceful, almost like I had been drugged. But I could still think clearly and see everything. We were in some sort of narrow, round tunnel. It seemed to circle the whole Opera House underground. I had once been in the cellars, but only down to the third level. There are two more below that—big enough for a whole village! I ran away the first time I went down there because I saw terrifying figures—like demons, dressed in black, standing before huge boilers, shoveling fire and opening furnace doors that glowed red. They scared me so much, I ran.

"Now, riding on César's back, I saw those same shadowy shapes far off in the distance, tiny in front of the fire. They flickered in and out of view as we moved. But then we passed them, and they disappeared completely.

"The man kept holding me steady. César walked on by himself, slow but steady. I don't know how long we traveled, but it felt endless. We kept turning and even went down spiral staircases—deeper and deeper, into the earth.

"At one point, César lifted his head and sniffed the air. He sped up a little. The air felt damp. Then we stopped. The darkness had faded slightly. A soft blue light glowed around us. We were at the edge of a lake—dark, heavy water that stretched out into the shadows. But the light let me see a small boat tied to a ring on the stone shore."

"A boat?" Raoul asked.

"Yes, and I knew this underground lake and boat were real, not magic. But Raoul, think about how I got there—on the back of a horse, in total darkness! I don't know if the drug he gave me had worn off, but my fear returned the moment he lifted me off the horse and into the boat.

"He sent César away—I heard the horse's hooves climbing stairs—and then the man jumped in beside me. He untied the rope and picked up the oars. He rowed quickly, strongly, and his eyes—hidden behind that mask—never stopped staring at me.

"We crossed the water in that strange blue glow, then slipped into darkness again before reaching the other shore. He picked me up again. I screamed. But then I stopped, completely stunned.

"We had entered a room full of bright light. I looked around, completely shocked. I was standing in the middle of what looked like a parlor, beautifully decorated with flowers. But the flowers were too perfect, too arranged—like something out of a store window, tied with ribbons like the kind in gift shops. They were too fake, too fancy, like the ones I found in my dressing room after a big show.

"In the middle of all that, stood the man in the black cloak and mask, arms folded across his chest. And he said to me, 'Don't be afraid, Christine. You're safe now.'

"It was the voice."

I was just as angry as I was shocked. I rushed toward him and tried to pull off the mask, desperate to see the face behind the voice. But he stopped me. He said, "You're safe—as long as you don't touch the mask." Then, gently, he took my wrists, guided me to a chair, and knelt before me in silence.

The way he humbled himself gave me back some of my courage. And the light in the room brought me back to reality. No matter how strange this whole experience was, I was now surrounded by normal, physical things: furniture, candles, curtains, baskets of flowers. I could even guess where those flowers came from and how much they cost. It all made the moment feel less like a dream and more like just a strange part of everyday life—even if it was happening five stories below the Opera House.

I realized then that the voice I had heard so many times was not just a voice—it was a man. He was kneeling in front of me. And I started to cry. He must have understood why, because he said, "It's true, Christine... I'm not an angel, or a genius, or a ghost. I'm Erik."

Just as I said his name, we heard it echoed back—"Erik." Raoul and I turned around quickly. Night had fallen. Raoul moved like he was about to stand up, but I stopped him.

"Don't go," I said. "You need to hear everything, right here."

"Why here, Christine? You'll catch cold."

"We're safe here. We're far away from the trapdoors. And I'm not allowed to see you anywhere else. We can't risk him finding out—not now."

"Christine," Raoul said anxiously, "something tells me we shouldn't wait until tomorrow night. We need to run away now."

"If I don't sing tomorrow," I said softly, "it will break his heart."

Raoul frowned. "It's hard to avoid hurting him if we want to escape for good."

"You're right," I said. "If I leave, it could kill him." Then, in a dull, lifeless tone, I added, "But he could kill us too."

"He loves you that much?" Raoul asked.

"He would do anything for me," I said. "Even something awful."

"Then we'll find where he lives," Raoul said. "Now that we know he's not a ghost, we can talk to him, force him to stop."

I shook my head. "No. You can't reason with Erik. The only choice is to escape."

"Then why did you go back to him when you had the chance to be free?"

"Because I had to. You'll understand when I tell you how I left him."

Raoul clenched his fists. "I hate him!" he shouted. "And you—Christine, do you hate him too?"

"No," I answered softly.

Raoul's face twisted in pain. "Of course not. You love him. That's what this is. You're afraid of him because you love him. That strange, twisted love that people don't want to admit even to themselves." His voice turned bitter. "You love a man who lives in an underground palace!"

I looked at him with cold eyes. "So, do you want me to go back there?" I asked harshly. "Because if I do... I may never come back."

Then there was silence. It felt like even the shadows around us were listening.

"Before I answer," Raoul said slowly, "I want to know how you really feel about him—since you say you don't hate him."

"I feel nothing but horror," I said. "And that's what makes it so hard. I'm horrified by him, and yet... I don't hate him. How could I? Imagine Erik, kneeling at my feet in that strange house by the lake. He cursed himself, begged me for forgiveness. He admitted everything. He said he loved me."

My voice grew shaky.

"He took me underground because he loved me. He trapped me there—because of love. But he never hurt me. He respected me. He cried, Raoul. He sobbed like a broken man. When I stood up and told him that I would only ever despise him if he didn't let me go right then, he agreed. He said he would show me the way out..."

I paused.

"But then he stood up, too. And I remembered that, even if he wasn't an angel or a ghost or some kind of genius—he was still the voice. He began to sing. And I listened. And I stayed.

"That night, we didn't say another word. He just sang me to sleep."

When I woke up, I was alone, lying on a couch in a small, plain bedroom. There was a simple wooden bed and a lamp on top of an old dresser. It looked like an ordinary room. But I quickly realized I was trapped. The only other door led to a bathroom. When I came back into the bedroom, I saw a note on the dresser written in red ink. It said:

"My dear Christine, you don't need to worry. You have no better or more respectful friend in the world than me. For now, you're alone in this home that belongs to you. I'm out shopping to get you everything you'll need."

That's when I knew I was dealing with someone who wasn't right in the head. I searched the room, hoping to find a way out, but there was none. I felt so foolish for believing in the "voice" and falling into this trap. I didn't know whether to laugh or cry.

That's when Erik appeared. He knocked three times on the wall, and a hidden door opened. He walked in calmly, his arms full of boxes and bags, and began placing them on the bed. I shouted at him, called him names, and demanded he take off his mask—if he really was an honest man. He replied calmly, "You'll never see Erik's face." Then he scolded me for not being dressed yet and told me it was already two in the afternoon. He even wound up my watch and reset it.

He invited me to join him for lunch in the dining room. I was furious, slammed the door on him, and stormed off to the bathroom. After a while, I came out feeling a little better. He said he loved me— but only when I let him say it—and that the rest of the time would be for music.

"What do you mean, 'the rest of the time'?" I asked.

"Five days," he answered firmly. I asked if I'd be free after that, and he said, "Yes, Christine. After five days, you'll learn not to see me. And then, from time to time, you'll come back to visit your poor Erik."

He pointed to a chair at a small table. I sat down, confused and uneasy. Still, I ate a few prawns, a bit of chicken, and half a glass of wine he said came from a famous cellar. Erik didn't eat or drink. I asked where he was from and if his name meant he was Scandinavian. He said he had no real name or country and just picked "Erik" by chance.

After lunch, he stood up and lightly touched my hand, saying he wanted to show me his home. But his hand felt cold and bony—it reminded me of death—and I pulled away, frightened. "I'm sorry," he said sadly and opened a door. "This is my bedroom. Would you like to see it? It's unusual."

His tone gave me some confidence, so I followed. The room looked like it belonged to someone dead. The walls were covered in black cloth, and instead of white trim, there was sheet music with the same line repeated from the Dies Irae, a funeral hymn. In the middle of the room was a canopy bed, and under the canopy was an open coffin.

"That's where I sleep," Erik said. "You have to get used to everything in life... even eternity."

It was too much for me—I turned away. Then I noticed a huge organ on one wall. A music book sat open with strange red notes. It was titled Don Juan Triumphant.

"Yes," Erik said. "I wrote that. I started twenty years ago. When it's finished, I'll take it into that coffin and never wake up again."

"You should take your time finishing it," I replied.

"Sometimes I work on it for two straight weeks without eating or sleeping. Then I won't touch it again for years," he said. I asked him to play a part of it, thinking it would make him happy.

"Never ask me that," he said in a dark voice. "I'll play Mozart instead—it'll only make you cry. But Don Juan burns with a fire that doesn't come from Heaven."

We returned to the other room. I noticed there were no mirrors anywhere. I was going to ask about it, but Erik had already sat down at the piano.

"You see, Christine," he said, "some music is so powerful it burns anyone who hears it. You haven't heard that kind yet. If you did, you'd lose all the color in your face, and no one would recognize you when you returned to Paris. Let's sing something from the Opera."

He said those last words like he was mocking me.

"What did you do?" Raoul asked.

"I didn't even have time to think about what he meant. We started the duet from Othello. I sang Desdemona with more pain and fear than I'd ever felt. His voice, full of fury and jealousy, thundered through the room. His black mask made me think of the real Othello. It was like he was Othello.

"And then... I had to see what was under that mask. I couldn't help it. I reached out and tore it off."

Christine paused, trembling.

"What I saw... oh, it was horrible. Truly horrible."

The dark sky above them echoed her words:

"Horror... Horror... Horror..."

Raoul and Christine held each other tightly as they looked up at the quiet, starry sky.

"It's strange," Raoul said softly, "that such a calm night could feel so full of sadness. It's like the sky itself is grieving."

"When you know the truth," Christine whispered, "you'll hear it too—the crying, always crying."

She gripped Raoul's hands and shivered as she continued.

"If I live to be a hundred, I'll still hear the awful scream he let out. It was a mix of heartbreak and rage, not human. Raoul, you've seen skulls before—maybe even his, when you thought you saw it at Perros, or when he was dressed as the Red Death at the masked ball. But those skulls were lifeless. His face was alive. Imagine a skull's empty eyes, nose, and mouth suddenly moving, twisting—full of fury like a demon. And the most terrifying part? His eyes don't even glow... not unless you're in complete darkness."

When I fell back against the wall, he came toward me, grinding his teeth in rage. I dropped to my knees, and he leaned over me, shouting nonsense and curses. He screamed, "Look! You wanted to see me— then look! Stare all you want at how disgusting I am! Feast your eyes on Erik's face! So the voice wasn't enough for you, huh? You had to see what I looked like. Oh, you women are always so curious! Well, are you satisfied now? Do you think I'm handsome? Because once a woman sees me, she belongs to me forever. They all do. I'm like Don Juan!"

Then he stood up tall, one hand on his hip, his horrible head swaying, and yelled, "Look at me! I am Don Juan Triumphant!"

I turned my head away and begged him to stop. But he grabbed my face, twisting his bony fingers into my hair.

"That's enough!" Raoul shouted. "I'll kill him! Christine, where is the lake dining room? Tell me—I'll kill him!"

"Be quiet, Raoul, if you really want to hear the rest."

"I do want to know—how and why you went back. I have to know! But no matter what, I'm going to kill him!"

"Raoul, listen! He dragged me by the hair and then… then… Oh, it was too awful…"

"What? Tell me!" Raoul demanded.

"He hissed at me, 'Oh, you're scared, are you? You think this is just another mask, don't you? Go ahead! Tear this one off too! Do it! I insist!' Then he grabbed my hands and forced them onto his face. He made me scratch his skin. I could feel it—dead, awful skin. 'You see?' he shouted. 'I'm made of death from head to toe! I'm just a corpse that loves you, worships you, and will never leave you! You tore off my mask, and now you can never leave me! When you thought I was handsome, you might've come back… but now that you've seen me, you'd run away forever. So now I'll keep you here! You wanted to see me, Christine! You wanted to see what not even my father saw! My own mother gave me my first mask so she wouldn't have to look at me!'"

Finally, he let go of me and crawled away like a snake, sobbing horribly. He locked himself in his room. Then I heard the organ begin to play. And that's when I started to understand why he always spoke about opera music with such disgust. This music was nothing like what I'd ever heard before. His Don Juan Triumphant was like one long, powerful cry—beautiful and painful all at once.

Then I understood every feeling inside him: suffering, longing, rage. It overwhelmed me. I opened the door between us. Erik stood up but didn't dare look at me.

"Erik," I said, "don't be afraid. Show me your face. I promise, I think you are the saddest and most amazing man I've ever known. If I flinch when I see you again, it'll only be because I'm moved by your brilliance."

He believed me. I believed myself. He collapsed at my feet, saying words of love from his cold, dead mouth. The music stopped. He kissed the edge of my dress, not realizing that I had closed my eyes.

What more can I say? Now you know the truth. The nightmare went on for two whole weeks. For that entire time, I lied to him. My lies were as twisted as he was, but they were the only way I could earn my freedom.

I burned his mask. I acted sweet and loyal, even when he wasn't singing. He started watching me like a dog watching its owner. He did everything to please me. Slowly, he trusted me enough to take me for walks by the lake, even boat rides. Toward the end of that time, he took me through a hidden gate into the Rue Scribe. A carriage waited there, and we went to the Bois.

That night when we ran into you, Raoul, was nearly fatal. He's terribly jealous of you. I had to lie and tell him you'd be leaving soon.

After all that—after two weeks filled with fear, sympathy, amazement, and sorrow—I told him, "I will come back." And he believed me.

"And you did go back," Raoul said in a low voice.

"Yes, and not because he threatened me. It was because of the heartbreaking sob he let out when I left. That cry touched me deeper than I realized. Poor Erik… poor Erik."

Raoul stood. "You say you love me, Christine. But just hours after you escaped, you returned to him. Don't forget the masked ball!"

"I haven't forgotten," she said. "And do you remember the hours I spent with you that night? Risking everything for us both?"

"Even then, I doubted your love for me."

"Do you still doubt me, Raoul?" she asked quietly. "Then listen—each time I visited Erik, my fear grew stronger. Each time, instead of calming down, he became more desperate and more obsessed. And I'm terrified, Raoul. So afraid…"

"You're afraid—but do you love me? If Erik were handsome, would you still love me?"

She stood up, wrapped her shaking arms around Raoul's neck, and whispered:

"Oh, my fiancé for just one day… if I didn't love you, I wouldn't let you kiss me. Take my kiss—just this once. It will be the first and the last."

He kissed her, but suddenly the peaceful night around them felt like it had been torn apart. A sense of fear rushed in, as if a storm was coming. They pulled away and looked up, terrified of Erik.

Above them, they saw a giant dark shape—like a bird of the night—watching with glowing eyes. It clung high above, seeming to rest on the string of Apollo's lyre, staring down at them.

Chapter XIII
A Master-Stroke of the Trap-Door Lover

Raoul and Christine ran as fast as they could, trying to escape from the rooftop and those terrifying glowing eyes that only appeared in the dark. They didn't stop until they reached the eighth floor on their way down.

The Opera was empty that night—there was no show, and the hallways were quiet. Suddenly, a strange-looking figure stepped in front of them, blocking their path.

"Not this way," the figure said, pointing toward another hallway that led to the wings of the stage.

Raoul started to ask who he was, but the figure—dressed in a long coat and a pointed cap—urged them, "Go! Quickly!"

Christine had already grabbed Raoul's hand and was pulling him forward again.

"Who is that man?" Raoul asked.

"It's the Persian," Christine whispered.

"What's he doing here?"

"No one really knows. He's always around the Opera."

"This is the first time in my life I've run from anyone," Raoul said. "If that really was Erik we saw up there, I should've climbed up to Apollo's lyre and nailed him there, like they do with owls on farmhouses back home."

Christine shook her head. "You'd have to climb up to that lyre first—and that's no easy job."

"But I saw those blazing eyes!"

"You're starting to sound like me now," she said. "You see him everywhere. What you thought were his eyes were probably just stars shining through the strings of the lyre."

They reached another floor and kept going.

"If you've truly decided to leave, Christine, I say we go now. Why wait until tomorrow? He may have heard us tonight."

"No, no," she insisted. "He's busy working on Don Juan Triumphant. He's not thinking about us."

"You're so sure, yet you keep looking behind you."

"Come with me to my dressing room."

"Wouldn't it be safer to meet outside the Opera?"

"Never—at least, not until we leave forever. I made him a promise that I'd only see you inside the Opera."

"Well, I'm lucky he even allowed that," Raoul muttered. "It was pretty bold of you to let us pretend we were engaged."

"He knows all about it," Christine said. "He told me, 'I trust you, Christine. M. de Chagny loves you and is going abroad. Let him be happy before he leaves—just as I am.'"

"Is love really supposed to make people so miserable?" Raoul asked.

"Yes, Raoul—when you love someone and don't know if they love you back."

They finally reached Christine's dressing room.

"Why do you think you're safer here than on the stage?" Raoul asked. "You heard him through these walls before—he can probably still hear us."

"No," she said. "He promised not to spy on me here anymore. I trust Erik's word. This room, and the bedroom by the lake, are mine. He swore not to come into them."

"But how did you go from this room into that hidden hallway? Can we try to follow your steps?"

"It's dangerous," she warned. "The mirror might take me again, and then I'd have no choice but to go all the way to the lake and call for Erik."

"Would he hear you?"

"Erik hears me no matter where I am. He told me that himself. He's not just some man who decided to live underground. He knows things no one else does."

"Careful," Raoul said. "You're starting to talk like he's a ghost again."

"No, he's not a ghost. He's just... part of both Heaven and Earth."

"Part of Heaven and Earth? That's all? That's how you describe him? And you still plan to run from him?"

"Yes. Tomorrow."

"Tomorrow, you might not have the strength to go through with it."

"Then you'll have to take me anyway—even if I resist. Promise me that."

"I'll be here at midnight. I gave you my word. So after the performance, he'll be waiting for you by the lake?"

"Yes."

"And how will you get there if you don't use the mirror?"

"I'll go to the lake another way."

Christine opened a box and showed him a large key.

"What's that?" Raoul asked.

"It unlocks the gate to the underground passage on Rue Scribe."

"So that's how you'll get there? Give the key to me, Christine."

"Never," she said firmly. "That would be betrayal."

Suddenly, Christine's face went pale. All the color drained from her skin.

"Oh no..." she whispered. "Erik! Erik! Please have mercy!"

"Be quiet!" Raoul warned. "You told me he can hear everything!"

But Christine looked more panicked than ever. She twisted her hands together and kept whispering:

"Oh no... oh Heaven... oh no!"

"What is it? What's wrong?" Raoul asked, frightened.

"The ring... the gold ring he gave me."

"So... it was Erik who gave you that ring?"

"You know he gave it to me, Raoul! But what you don't know is what he said when he gave it. He told me, 'I'm giving you your freedom back, Christine—but only if you always wear this ring. As long as you keep it on, you'll be safe, and Erik will remain your friend. But if you ever lose it, he'll take revenge.' Raoul... the ring is gone! We're both in danger now!"

They searched everywhere but couldn't find it. Christine was frantic.

"It must've slipped off my finger when I kissed you under Apollo's lyre," she cried. "It probably fell into the street. We'll never find it now. Who knows what's going to happen to us! Oh, we need to run away!"

"Let's go right now," Raoul urged again.

She paused. He thought she was about to agree... but then her eyes lost their sparkle and she whispered, "No. Tomorrow."

She hurried away, still rubbing her fingers like she thought she could magically bring the ring back.

Raoul went home, deeply troubled by everything she had said.

"If I don't save her from that lunatic," he muttered aloud, "she's doomed. But I will save her."

He turned off the lamp and lay in bed. In the darkness, he suddenly felt the urge to curse Erik.

"Humbug! Humbug! Humbug!" he shouted into the night.

But then he froze. A cold sweat broke out on his forehead.

Two eyes—bright and burning like fire—appeared at the foot of his bed, staring at him silently in the dark.

Raoul wasn't a coward, but his body trembled. Slowly, he reached toward the table for the matches. His fingers found them, struck one, and lit the candle.

The eyes vanished.

Still uneasy, he thought, She told me his eyes only appear in the dark. They disappeared in the light... but maybe he's still here.

He got out of bed, searched the room, even looked under the bed like a scared child. Feeling silly, he got back into bed and blew out the candle.

The eyes came back.

Raoul sat up and stared straight at them, doing his best to stay brave.

"Is that you, Erik? Are you a man? A genius? A ghost?"

Then he thought, If it really is him, he must be on the balcony.

He got up, found his revolver in the drawer, opened the window, and looked out. No one was there. He shut the window, shivering from the cold, and returned to bed. He placed the gun beside him, within reach.

The eyes were still there.

He tried to figure it out—were they inside the room or just outside the glass? He needed answers. Carefully, he picked up the revolver, aimed just above the eyes, and fired.

The blast shattered the silence of the night. Footsteps rushed through the house. Raoul stayed sitting up, arm outstretched, ready to shoot again if needed.

But this time, the eyes were gone.

Servants ran in with lights. Count Philippe appeared, looking frightened.

"What happened?"

"I think I was dreaming," Raoul said. "I shot at two stars that wouldn't let me sleep."

"You're not making any sense! Are you sick?" Philippe cried, grabbing the revolver. "What happened?"

"We'll know soon enough," Raoul said calmly.

He got out of bed, threw on his robe and slippers, took a candle from a servant, and stepped onto the balcony.

The count followed. He saw that a bullet had gone through the window at about head height. Raoul leaned over the balcony with the light.

"Aha," he said quietly. "Blood. There's blood here... and here... more of it! That's good. A ghost that bleeds isn't as scary."

He actually smiled.

"Raoul! Raoul! Raoul!" the count cried, grabbing his shoulders like he was trying to wake someone from a dream.

"But, Philippe, I'm not dreaming!" Raoul said, frustrated. "You saw the blood yourself! At first, I thought I was imagining things and shooting at stars. But those were Erik's eyes... and this is his blood! Maybe I shouldn't have fired, and Christine might never forgive me... None of this would've happened if I'd just closed the curtains before bed."

"Raoul, have you lost your mind?" Philippe said. "Wake up!"

"You still don't believe me? You'd be more helpful if you helped me find Erik. A ghost that bleeds can't be that hard to track down."

One of the servants said, "He's right, sir. There's definitely blood on the balcony."

Another servant brought a lamp, and they examined the area. The blood trail ran along the railing, then disappeared up the gutter.

"My dear brother," Philippe said, "you must have shot a cat."

Raoul gave a strange grin. "Maybe. With Erik, you never really know. It could've been Erik. It could've been a cat. It could've been the ghost. You just never know."

Raoul kept rambling, saying things that matched the confused state of his mind. His words were so strange and intense that even the police report later said he sounded unstable. Philippe started to believe it too. And when the investigating judge read the report later, he came to the same conclusion.

"Who is Erik?" Philippe asked, holding his brother's hand.

"He's my rival. And if he's still alive, that's a shame."

He waved the servants away, and the two brothers were left alone. But the valet hadn't gone far and clearly heard Raoul say:

"I'm taking Christine Daaé away tonight."

That exact phrase would later be repeated to the judge. No one ever found out exactly what was said between the brothers after that. But the servants claimed it wasn't the first time they'd argued, and it was always about Christine Daaé.

Later that morning, during breakfast in Philippe's study, he called for Raoul. Raoul came in silent and grim. Philippe handed him a copy of L'Époque and said, "Read this."

Raoul read the headline:

"Big News in the Faubourg: A rumored engagement between the rising opera star Christine Daaé and Vicomte Raoul de Chagny has society talking. Sources say Count Philippe de Chagny strongly opposes the match and has sworn to stop it—an unusual move for a Chagny. But in matters of love, especially at the Opera, it's love, not family, that usually wins."

"You see?" Philippe said. "You're making the whole family look like fools. That girl has completely messed with your head and filled it with ghost stories."

Raoul had clearly told his brother everything Christine had said the night before. Now, all he said was:

"Goodbye, Philippe."

"You've really made up your mind? You're leaving tonight? With her?"

Raoul didn't answer.

"You can't seriously be thinking of doing something so reckless. I will stop you."

"Goodbye, Philippe," Raoul repeated, and he left.

Later, Count Philippe told the same story to the judge. It was the last time he saw Raoul until that night at the Opera, just minutes before Christine disappeared.

Raoul spent the whole day preparing to run away with Christine. He arranged for horses, a carriage, a driver, packed their things, gathered the money they'd need, and planned out their route. He decided not to take the train so Erik wouldn't be able to follow them. All these preparations kept him busy until nine o'clock that night.

At nine o'clock, a covered carriage rolled up near the Rotunda entrance of the Opera House. The windows were curtained shut. Two strong horses pulled it, driven by a coachman with most of his face hidden under a thick scarf. Parked ahead of it were three smaller carriages—one for Carlotta, who had just returned to Paris, another for Sorelli, and the first for Count Philippe de Chagny. No one stepped

152

out of the mysterious carriage. All the coachmen, including the one for the hidden barouche, stayed quietly in place.

Then, a shadowy figure in a long black cloak and a soft black hat walked along the sidewalk. It paused near the carriage, looked closely at it, inspected the horses and the driver, then walked away without saying anything. Some later believed this shadow was Raoul, but that seems unlikely—Raoul always wore a tall top hat, which was found later. It's more believable that it was the Opera Ghost, who seemed to know everything that was about to happen.

That night, Faust was playing to a full house. Many from high society were there, especially since the morning newspaper had hinted at an engagement between Christine Daaé and Vicomte Raoul de Chagny. Count Philippe sat alone in his box, trying to appear calm and uninterested, but everyone kept glancing in his direction. The women in the audience whispered behind their fans, surprised that Raoul wasn't there. Christine entered to a cool welcome. Some people in the audience clearly disapproved of her aiming so high in love.

Christine noticed the cold reaction and felt nervous. Her confidence wavered. Some regular opera-goers smirked knowingly during parts of her role as Margarita, especially during the lines:

"I just wish I knew who he was—

The one who spoke to me.

Was he someone important?

Or at least, what is his name?"

Every time she sang something like that, people would glance over at Count Philippe's box. He sat still with his chin resting on his hand, his eyes fixed on the stage, but his thoughts clearly elsewhere.

Christine became more and more unsettled. She looked like she might not make it through the performance. Carolus Fonta, her co-star, worried she was too sick to finish the Garden Scene. In the audience, people remembered when Carlotta had famously lost her voice in that same scene—and how it had nearly ruined her career.

Just then, Carlotta entered her box on the other side of the theater. It was dramatic and caught everyone's attention. Christine looked up and spotted her rival, who seemed to be smirking. That gave Christine the push she needed. She pulled herself together and poured her heart into the rest of the performance.

From then on, she sang beautifully—better than ever. In the final act, when she began her angelic song, it felt like she lifted the entire audience with her voice.

Then, right in the middle of that magical moment, something incredible happened.

Christine sang:

"Holy angel, in Heaven blessed…"

And then, with her arms stretched out and her golden hair falling across her shoulders, she sang the last line:

"My spirit longs with thee to rest!"

At that exact moment, the stage lights went out. It was so sudden, no one had time to react. Then, just as quickly, the lights came back on.

But Christine was gone.

She had vanished right in front of thousands of eyes.

Everyone froze in shock. People looked at each other in confusion. The noise in the theater rose to chaos. On stage, performers and crew ran to where she had just been standing. The show couldn't go on.

Where was Christine? How could she disappear into thin air like that? It was like the angels had really come to carry her away, just as the song said.

Raoul, who had been standing in the audience, cried out. Count Philippe jumped to his feet in his box. The audience started buzzing with questions. Was this somehow connected to the morning's newspaper article?

Raoul rushed out of his seat. Philippe left his box. As the curtain came down, audience members pushed toward the backstage doors. The rest sat frozen in a noisy blur of shock, gossip, and confusion.

Finally, the curtain rose again. Carolus Fonta stepped forward, walked to the conductor's podium, and in a serious tone said:

"Ladies and gentlemen, something has happened tonight unlike anything we've ever seen. Our fellow artist, Christine Daaé, has vanished before our very eyes—and no one knows how or why."

Chapter XIV
The Singular Attitude of a Safety-Pin

Behind the curtain, everything was in chaos. Performers, stage crew, dancers, extras, singers, and even some audience members were packed together, shouting and pushing each other in confusion.

"Where did she go?"

"She ran away!"

"She must've left with the Vicomte de Chagny!"

"No, it was the Count!"

"Carlotta's behind this!"

"No, it was the Phantom!" someone said, and a few people laughed—especially since they had already checked the trapdoors and floorboards and found no sign of an accident.

Away from the noise, three men stood in a corner, whispering and waving their arms as they tried to figure out what to do. They were Gabriel, the chorus master; Mercier, the acting manager; and Remy, the Opera's secretary. They gathered near the hallway that connects the stage to the ballet area, hiding behind some large props.

"I knocked on their office door," said Remy. "They didn't answer. Maybe they're not in there. And even if they are, we can't check—because they took the keys with them."

"They" were the theater managers. Before the last intermission, they told everyone they didn't want to be disturbed for any reason.

"Still," Gabriel said, clearly upset, "you don't just lose a singer in the middle of a show!"

"Did you tell them that?" Mercier asked, annoyed.

"I'll go knock again," Remy replied, then ran off.

Right then, the stage manager appeared.

"Well, M. Mercier, are you coming or not? What are you two waiting around for? They need you, Mr. Acting Manager!"

"I'm not doing anything else until the police get here," Mercier said. "I called for Commissary Mifroid. We'll wait for him to arrive before doing anything."

"I'm telling you, we should check the organ room right now."

"Not until the commissary gets here."

"I already went down there myself."

"Oh yeah? And what did you see?"

"Nothing! No one was there, I'm telling you—no one!"

"Then what's the point of me going down there?" Mercier asked.

"You're probably right," the stage manager said, running his fingers through his hair, clearly stressed. "But maybe someone near the organ knows how the lights went out so fast. And now we can't even find Mauclair!"

Mauclair was the man who ran the lights for the stage. He controlled when the lights changed from day to night and back again during the shows.

"Mauclair is missing?" Mercier asked again, shocked. "Then where are the people who help him?"

"There's no sign of Mauclair or his assistants!" the stage manager shouted. "Nobody's working the lights! Don't you get it? That girl didn't just disappear by magic—someone took her! This was all planned ahead of time! We need to find out who's behind it. And where are the managers while this is going on? I gave clear orders that no one was allowed near the lighting controls, and I even placed a fireman outside the gas room next to the organ. That was the right move, wasn't it?"

"Yes, yes, of course," said Mercier. "Now let's wait for the police."

The stage manager stormed off, shaking his head and muttering insults about everyone standing around doing nothing while the whole Opera was in total chaos.

Gabriel and Mercier weren't just standing around, though. They had been given strict orders not to disturb the managers no matter what. Remy had already broken that rule and gotten nowhere.

Just then, Remy came back looking shaken.

"Well? Did you talk to them?" Mercier asked.

"Moncharmin finally opened the door," Remy said. "His eyes were bulging like he was going to hit me. I tried to speak, but before I could say anything, he shouted, 'Do you have a safety pin?' I said no, and he yelled, 'Then go away!' I told him something serious had happened on stage, but he just screamed, 'A safety pin! Bring me a safety pin!' A boy heard him, ran over, and handed him one. Moncharmin snatched it and slammed the door in my face."

"You didn't say 'Christine Daaé'?" Mercier asked.

"I would love to see you try in that situation! The man looked ready to have a breakdown. If that kid hadn't shown up with the pin, I think he might've fainted! None of this makes sense. Our managers are acting like they've lost their minds! And I'm not used to being treated like that!"

Suddenly, Gabriel whispered, "It's another one of the Phantom's tricks."

Remy gave a half-laugh. Mercier sighed, about to speak—but when Gabriel looked at him, he kept quiet.

Still, as time went on with no sign of the managers, Mercier started to feel the pressure.

"I'm going to find them myself!" he finally said.

Gabriel suddenly turned serious. "Be careful, Mercier. If they're staying in their office, there might be a reason. The Phantom has a lot of tricks."

Mercier shook his head. "That's their problem. I'm going. If anyone had listened to me earlier, the police would already know everything!"

And off he went.

"What 'everything'?" Remy asked. "What should the police know? Gabriel, why won't you say anything? Don't make me shout that all of you have gone insane! Because that's how it looks!"

Gabriel just gave a clueless look. "What are you talking about? What do you think I know?"

Remy was clearly losing patience.

"Tonight, between the acts, Richard and Moncharmin were acting completely crazy!"

"I didn't notice anything," Gabriel said, frowning. He was clearly annoyed now too.

"You must be the only one who didn't notice! Do you think I didn't see it? Or that Mr. Parabise, the Credit Central manager, missed it? Or the ambassador, Mr. de La Borderie, didn't see anything either? Everyone in the audience was pointing at our managers!"

"So, what were the managers doing?" Gabriel asked, acting like he had no idea.

"What were they doing? Come on—you know exactly what! You were standing right there with Mercier, watching them. You two were the only ones who didn't laugh!"

"I really don't know what you're talking about," Gabriel said, shrugging like it wasn't important. But Remy kept going.

"Why are they acting so strange now? Why don't they want anyone near them anymore?"

"What? They're avoiding people now?"

"And they won't even let anyone touch them!"

"Really? You've actually seen that? That's pretty weird."

"Oh, so now you admit it! Took you long enough! And they've even started walking backward!"

"Walking backward? You're serious? What are they, crabs?" Gabriel joked.

"This isn't funny, Gabriel. Cut it out."

"I'm not joking," Gabriel said, putting on a serious face.

"Then explain something. When I walked up to Mr. Richard during the garden scene and held out my hand to say hello, why did Mr. Moncharmin jump in and whisper, 'Don't touch the director!'? Do I look sick or something?"

"That's insane!"

"And later, when the ambassador tried to talk to Richard, didn't you see Moncharmin step in again and beg him not to touch the director?"

"That's just bizarre! What did Richard do then?"

"You saw it! He turned around, bowed to thin air, and started walking away—backward!"

"Backward?"

"And Moncharmin followed behind, walking in a half-circle and going backward too. They walked like that all the way to their office—backward the whole way! If that's not crazy, then what is it?"

"Maybe they were practicing a ballet move," Gabriel said weakly.

Remy frowned, clearly annoyed by the joke. He leaned in and whispered in Gabriel's ear:

"Stop pretending, Gabriel. You and Mercier know something you're not telling."

"What are you getting at?" Gabriel asked.

"Christine Daaé isn't the only one who vanished tonight."

"Oh, give me a break!"

"I'm serious. If that's not true, then why did Mercier grab Mother Giry's hand and rush her off when she came down to the foyer just now?"

"I didn't see that."

"Yes, you did, Gabriel. You went with them to Mercier's office. Since then, people have seen you and Mercier—but no one's seen her."

"What, do you think we ate her or something?"

"No, but you definitely locked her in that office. Anyone walking past can hear her shouting, 'Those scoundrels! Those scoundrels!'"

Right then, Mercier showed up, out of breath.

"It's worse than we thought," he said in a low, serious voice. "I yelled, 'This is urgent! Open the door! It's me, Mercier!' I heard someone walking, then Moncharmin opened the door. He looked really pale and asked, 'What do you want?' I told him, 'Christine Daaé has been taken!' And do you know what he said? 'Well, good!' Then he shut the door after handing me this."

Mercier held out his hand. Remy and Gabriel leaned in to look.

"A safety pin!" Remy exclaimed.

"This is so strange... really strange," Gabriel muttered, giving an involuntary shiver.

Just then, a voice behind them made all three turn around.

"Excuse me, gentlemen. Do you know where Christine Daaé is?"

Even though the situation was serious, the question might have made them laugh—if not for the heartbreaking look on the speaker's face. It was Raoul, the Vicomte de Chagny.

Chapter XV
Christine! Christine!

After Christine Daaé's strange and sudden disappearance, Raoul immediately blamed Erik. He now fully believed that the so-called Angel of Music had incredible, almost magical power in the world of the Opera, where he ruled in secret. Overcome with love and panic, Raoul rushed onto the stage.

"Christine! Christine!" he cried out, thinking she must be calling out to him from somewhere deep beneath the Opera where the Phantom had taken her. "Christine!"

He imagined he could hear her screaming from below the stage. He leaned down and listened, pacing the stage like a madman. He desperately wanted to go down into the darkness—but no one was allowed in the lower levels that night. All the doors to the underground were locked.

"Christine! Christine… are you there? Are you alive?"

Terrible thoughts ran through Raoul's mind. Erik must have found out that Christine had betrayed him. He must have known about their plan to run away. Raoul remembered the two glowing yellow eyes he saw the night before outside his window. Why hadn't he acted then? Some people had eyes that glowed in the dark—like cats or certain animals. Maybe Erik was like that. Maybe he'd been planning something all along. Raoul had fired his gun… but he hadn't stopped him. Erik had escaped, like a cat climbing up a drainpipe, and had gone after Christine instead.

These haunting thoughts filled Raoul's mind as he ran to Christine's dressing room.

"Christine! Christine!"

His heart broke as he looked around the room and saw her clothes—the ones she had laid out for their escape. He cursed the fact that she had refused to leave earlier. Why had she taken such a risk? Why had she hesitated, tried to be kind to a monster? Why had she sung that final, beautiful song as a gift to him?

Raoul, choked with tears, curses, and sorrow, fumbled at the mirror that had once opened to let Christine into Erik's underground world. He pushed it, searched for a latch, whispered, begged—nothing worked. Maybe you had to say special words? He remembered hearing that some things only obeyed commands spoken out loud.

Then he remembered the secret passage that led to the Rue Scribe. Christine had told him about it—the underground tunnel that went from the lake to the street. He checked the box where the key had once been, but it was gone. Still, he raced out to the Rue Scribe and searched along the wall, feeling every stone, trying to find a door. He touched metal bars—was this it? Or maybe over here? He peered through an air vent. It was pitch black. He pressed his face to the bars, straining to see or hear something… anything.

He circled the building and found a huge set of gates. It was the entrance to the Opera's administration courtyard. He ran into the doorkeeper's lodge.

"Please, ma'am, do you know of a gate or door with iron bars that opens into the Rue Scribe? One that leads to the lake beneath the Opera?"

"Yes, sir," she said, "I've heard there's a lake under the Opera, but I don't know how to get to it. I've never seen it."

"What about the Rue Scribe? Surely you've been there?"

The woman burst out laughing. Raoul, frustrated and furious, ran out again, stormed through the back areas of the Opera, up and down staircases, until he found himself back on stage.

His heart jumped—what if Christine had been found?

He saw a group of men talking and asked quickly, "Excuse me, gentlemen. Do you know where Christine Daaé is?"

Someone laughed.

Then there was a new buzz of voices, and through a crowd of fancy-dressed men came someone calm and smiling—a round-faced man with rosy cheeks and clear blue eyes. Mercier, the acting manager, leaned toward Raoul and said:

"That's the man you want to talk to. This is Monsieur Mifroid, the police commissary."

"Ah! The Vicomte de Chagny?" said Mifroid politely. "Pleased to meet you, sir. Would you come with me? Now—where are the managers?"

Mercier didn't answer, but Remy, the secretary, stepped forward.

"They're locked in their office. They don't know anything yet."

"You don't say! Let's go see them."

With more people joining them, M. Mifroid led the way to the managers' office. Mercier slipped a key to Gabriel and whispered:

"This is turning into a disaster. You'd better go let Mother Giry out."

Gabriel nodded and left.

Soon, they reached the office door. Mercier banged on it, but no one answered.

"Open up in the name of the law!" Mifroid shouted, his voice loud and serious.

Finally, the door opened. Everyone rushed into the office, right behind the police commissary.

Raoul was the last one to step inside. Just as he was about to enter, he felt a hand on his shoulder and heard a quiet voice whisper in his ear:

"Erik's secrets belong to him alone."

Raoul spun around with a shocked gasp. The hand on his shoulder now moved to cover the lips of the man who had spoken. He had dark skin, piercing green eyes, and wore a fur-trimmed hat. It was the Persian.

The man kept his finger to his lips, silently asking Raoul to stay quiet. Just as Raoul was about to ask why he had stopped him, the mysterious stranger gave a small bow—and vanished.

Chapter XVI

Mme. Giry's Astounding Revelations as to Her Personal Relations with the Opera Ghost

Before we follow the police officer into the manager's office, I need to explain some strange events that happened there—events that Remy and Mercier tried but failed to witness. Richard and Moncharmin had locked themselves inside the office with a specific purpose that the reader doesn't yet know, but that I must now reveal.

Earlier, I mentioned that the managers' attitudes had changed for the worse lately. This wasn't just because of the chandelier crash during the gala. There was another reason.

The truth is, the Opera Ghost had already been paid his first 20,000 francs without any trouble. As shocking as it sounds, it happened very simply. One morning, the managers found an envelope on their desk labeled "To Monsieur O.G. (Private)" along with a note from the ghost himself:

The time has come to follow the agreement in the contract book. Please place twenty 1,000-franc notes in this envelope, seal it with your official stamp, and give it to Madame Giry. She will handle the rest.

The managers didn't waste time. Without even questioning how the ghost managed to get this message into their locked office, they saw it as their chance to catch him. They shared the whole story with Gabriel and Mercier, swearing them to secrecy. Then they placed the money into the envelope and handed it to Madame Giry, who had recently been allowed to return to her old job.

Madame Giry didn't seem surprised. Of course, she was closely watched. She went straight to Box Five, the ghost's box, and placed the envelope on the small shelf inside. The managers, along with Gabriel and Mercier, had hidden themselves nearby so they could watch the envelope the entire night. It never moved, and even after the performance ended, the envelope still sat untouched. Eventually, Madame Giry left, and the men remained hidden. Tired of waiting, they finally checked the envelope.

At first glance, it looked like the money was still there. But soon they saw that something was wrong. The real money had been replaced by twenty fake bills from a made-up place called the "Bank of St. Farce."

The managers were furious—and scared. Moncharmin wanted to call the police right away, but Richard stopped him.

"We'd just be laughed at," Richard said. "Let O.G. have this round. We'll win the next one."

He was thinking about the next month's payment.

Still, being tricked so easily left them feeling humiliated. Deep down, they even wondered if the whole thing was a cruel prank by the former managers—and they didn't want to bring that theory into the open too soon. At times, Moncharmin even suspected Richard might be behind it, since he sometimes had strange ideas. So they decided to wait and keep a close eye on Madame Giry. But Richard didn't want anyone to question her.

"If she's working with the ghost, then the money's already gone," he said. "But honestly, I think she's just a fool."

"She's not the only fool in this situation," Moncharmin said quietly.

"Well, who could've guessed it would turn out like this?" Richard groaned. "But don't worry. Next time, I'll be ready."

That "next time" came on the same day Christine Daaé disappeared. That morning, the ghost had sent another note:

Do the same thing as before. Everything went perfectly. Put the 20,000 francs in the envelope and give it to our excellent Madame Giry.

And as usual, the note came with the familiar envelope. All they had to do was put in the money.

About thirty minutes before the first act of Faust began, Richard showed the envelope to Moncharmin. He then counted out the twenty one-thousand-franc bills and placed them inside the envelope—without sealing it.

"Now," Richard said, "let's bring in Madame Giry."

The old woman was sent for. She entered with a deep, sweeping curtsy. She still wore her old black taffeta dress, which was now faded with shades of brown and purple, and the same worn-out bonnet. She seemed to be in a cheerful mood and said right away:

"Good evening, gentlemen! I assume this is about the envelope?"

"Yes, Madame Giry," Richard replied politely. "It's about the envelope—and something more."

"I'm happy to help, Mr. Richard. What else do you need?"

"First, Madame Giry, I have a little question for you."

"Of course, sir. I'm here to answer anything you ask."

"Are you still on good terms with the ghost?"

"Couldn't be better, sir. Couldn't be better."

"Ah, wonderful! Look, Madame Giry," Richard said, lowering his voice as though sharing a secret, "we might as well speak plainly … you're no fool."

"Why, thank you, sir," the box-keeper replied, stopping the gentle bobbing of her black bonnet feathers. "No one's ever said otherwise!"

"Exactly. So I think we'll understand each other quickly. This ghost story … it's all just nonsense, isn't it? Honestly now, just between us … it's gone on long enough."

Madame Giry looked at the two managers as if they were speaking a foreign language. She walked up to the desk and asked, worried:

"What are you trying to say? I don't understand."

"Oh, come on, you understand perfectly well. And if you don't, you'd better start. First, tell us his name."

"Whose name?"

"The man you're working with, Madame Giry!"

"Me? Working with the ghost? What for?"

"You do everything he tells you."

"Well, he's not very demanding."

"And he still pays you?"

"I've no complaints."

"How much does he give you for delivering that envelope?"

"Ten francs."

"You poor woman! That's not very much, is it?"

"Why?"

"We'll get to that in a moment. Right now, we want to know why you're so devoted to this ghost. A woman like you doesn't give her loyalty for just five or ten francs."

"That's true," she admitted. "And I can tell you why. There's nothing shameful about it … quite the opposite."

"We're sure of that, Madame Giry!"

"Well, here's how it happened … though the ghost doesn't like me talking about his business."

"Really?" Richard said, with a smirk.

"But this part is about me alone. One night, I found a letter in Box Five. It was addressed to me. It was written in red ink. I don't need to read it to you, sir—I know it by heart, and I'll never forget it, not even if I live to be a hundred!"

And then, standing a little taller, Madame Giry recited the letter with a proud, emotional voice:

Madame:

In 1825, Mademoiselle Menetrier, leader of the ballet, became the Marquise de Cussy.

1832: Mlle. Marie Taglioni, a ballerina, became Countess Gilbert des Voisins.

1846: La Sota, another dancer, married the brother of the King of Spain.

1847: Lola Montes, also a dancer, became the unofficial wife of King Louis of Bavaria and was given the title Countess of Landsfeld.

1848: Mlle. Maria, a dancer, became Baroness d'Herneville.

1870: Theresa Hessier, a dancer, married Dom Fernando, brother to the King of Portugal.

Richard and Moncharmin listened as Madame Giry listed these fancy marriages. She seemed to grow prouder and more confident with every name. Then, with her voice full of pride, she shouted the last line from the letter:

1885: Meg Giry, Empress!

Exhausted from the excitement, Madame Giry dropped into a chair and said, "Gentlemen, the letter was signed 'Opera Ghost.' I had heard a lot about the ghost, but I never fully believed in him. But the moment he said my Meg—my very own daughter—would become an empress, I believed him completely."

It wasn't hard to see how easily Madame Giry had been swept away by the words "ghost" and "empress." But the big question was: who was behind all this?

"You've never seen him, but he talks to you and you just believe everything he says?" asked Moncharmin.

"Yes! And he helped my little Meg become the leader of her row of dancers. I told the ghost, 'If she's going to be an empress in 1885, she needs to start moving up now!' And he said, 'Consider it done.' After that, he just had to whisper something to Mr. Poligny, and it happened."

"So Poligny saw him too?" Moncharmin asked.

"No, not exactly. He never saw him either—but he heard him. The ghost whispered in his ear the night he came out of Box Five looking pale as a sheet."

Moncharmin groaned. "This is all so insane!"

"I always thought Mr. Poligny had some sort of secret deal with the ghost," Madame Giry said. "Anytime the ghost asked for something, Mr. Poligny made sure it happened. He couldn't say no."

"You hear that, Richard?" Moncharmin said. "Poligny couldn't say no to the ghost."

"Yes, yes, I heard!" snapped Richard. "Poligny was friends with the ghost. And since Madame Giry is friends with Poligny, everything makes perfect sense! ... But I don't care about Poligny." His tone turned sharp. "The only one I care about right now is you, Madame Giry. Do you know what's inside this envelope?"

"Of course not," she said.

"Take a look."

Madame Giry peered inside the envelope. At first she looked uninterested, but then her eyes lit up.

"Thousand-franc notes!" she gasped.

"Yes, thousand-franc notes! And you already knew that!"

"Me? No, sir, I swear—"

"Don't bother swearing, Madame Giry! I'll tell you the second reason I brought you here. I'm having you arrested."

The two black feathers on her hat, which usually stood like question marks, now shot up like exclamation points. Her hat tilted forward angrily over her messy hair. With a burst of energy, she rushed forward, nearly crashing into Mr. Richard's desk. He had to push his chair back in alarm.

"Arrest me?!" she shouted.

Her mouth, missing most of its teeth, seemed to launch the words like weapons at Richard.

But Richard stood firm. He didn't back down. He pointed a firm finger, ready to accuse her to the police.

"I'm having you arrested, Madame Giry—as a thief!"

"Say that again!"

Before Moncharmin could stop her, Madame Giry smacked Richard across the face—but it wasn't her hand that hit him. It was the envelope—the very same one causing all the trouble. When it struck him, it popped open, and the banknotes inside flew out like a swirl of giant butterflies.

Both managers gasped and immediately dropped to their knees, frantically grabbing and checking the scattered bills.

"Are they still real, Moncharmin?"

"Are they real, Richard?"

"Yes, they're still real!"

Above them, Madame Giry stood shaking with rage, her few teeth clacking noisily as she repeated over and over:

"Me? A thief? A thief? Me?"

She choked on her anger. "I've never heard anything so ridiculous!"

Then she stormed up to Richard again. "And besides," she shouted, "you, Monsieur Richard, should know better than I do where the twenty thousand francs went!"

"Me?" Richard replied, stunned. "Why would I know?"

Moncharmin, now looking both serious and annoyed, jumped in. "What are you trying to say, Madame Giry? Why do you think Monsieur Richard knows more than you do about the missing money?"

Richard, whose face was now turning red, grabbed Madame Giry's wrist and shook it hard. His voice boomed like thunder:

"Why should I know more than you? Tell me—why?!"

"Because you're the one who ended up with the money in your pocket!" she gasped, glaring at him like he was the devil himself.

Richard lunged toward her, but Moncharmin held him back and quickly said, more calmly:

"Wait! Let her talk. Let me question her." Then he added, "This is amazing. We're about to solve the whole thing, and you're getting angry? Calm down—I'm actually enjoying this."

Madame Giry straightened up, like a proud martyr. Her face was full of confidence and belief in her innocence.

"You say there were twenty thousand francs in the envelope I put in Monsieur Richard's pocket. But I tell you again—I didn't know anything about it! And neither did Monsieur Richard!"

"Oh really?" Richard snapped, suddenly acting bold. "So I didn't know either? You put twenty thousand francs in my pocket and I didn't even notice? Well, thank you, Madame Giry!"

"Yes," she said firmly. "It's true. Neither of us knew. But eventually, you must have found out!"

Richard looked like he was about to explode, but Moncharmin stepped in again to protect her.

"What envelope did you put in Monsieur Richard's pocket?" he asked. "It wasn't the one we gave you—the one we watched you take to Box Five. That was the one that held the real money."

"Excuse me," said Madame Giry. "The envelope you gave me is the one I slipped into Monsieur Richard's pocket. The one I took to the ghost's box was a different one, exactly like it. The ghost gave it to me ahead of time, and I hid it in my sleeve."

She pulled out an identical envelope from her sleeve, already sealed and labeled like the first. The managers took it and inspected it. The seal was theirs—just like the real envelope. They opened it and found the same fake money from the Bank of St. Farce—the kind that had fooled them the month before.

"How simple!" Richard said.

"How simple!" Moncharmin repeated, staring at Madame Giry like he was trying to read her mind.

"So it was the ghost who gave you this envelope and told you to switch it with the one we gave you? And the ghost told you to slip the real one into Mr. Richard's pocket?"

"Yes, it was the ghost," she replied.

"Then could you give us a little demonstration? Here's the envelope—pretend we don't know anything."

"As you wish, gentlemen," said Madame Giry.

She took the envelope with the real money inside and headed toward the door. But just as she was about to walk out, both managers jumped up and blocked her way.

"Oh no! We're not falling for that again!" Richard shouted. "Fool us once, shame on us—fool us twice? Not happening!"

176

"Excuse me, gentlemen," said the old woman calmly. "You told me to act like you didn't know anything. Well, if that were really the case, I'd simply leave with the envelope."

"And how exactly would you get it into my pocket?" Richard challenged her.

Moncharmin, trying to keep an eye on both of them at once, squinted one eye at Richard and the other at Madame Giry. It wasn't easy, but he was determined to get to the bottom of this.

"I'm supposed to slip it in when you're not expecting it, sir," she said. "You know I often wander backstage in the evening, especially when I bring my daughter her ballet shoes. I'm allowed in the ballet foyer as her mother. There are always lots of people back there—subscribers, performers, managers... including you, sir. I just walk by and slip the envelope into your tailcoat pocket. Nothing magical about it."

"No magic?" Richard growled, his eyes flashing with anger. "No magic? I just caught you lying, you old witch!"

Madame Giry puffed up with anger, baring her few remaining teeth.

"And what lie would that be?"

"You said you gave me the envelope that same evening—but I never went near the ballet foyer that night! I was watching Box Five the entire time. I never left."

"No, sir," she corrected him, "I didn't give it to you that night. I gave it to you the next time, during the performance when the undersecretary of state for fine arts came."

At those words, Richard suddenly perked up.

"Yes! That's right—I remember now! The undersecretary asked to see me backstage. I stepped down to the ballet foyer for a minute. I was standing on the stairs... the undersecretary and his assistant were just inside. I turned around and—yes! You brushed past me, Madame Giry. I remember it clearly now!"

"Yes, sir, that's when it happened. I had just finished what I needed to do. That pocket of yours is really convenient."

And to prove it, Madame Giry walked behind Richard again and, with surprising speed, slipped the envelope into his coat pocket. Even Moncharmin had to admit he was impressed.

"Of course!" Richard said, turning a little pale. "That's how O.G. pulled it off! His goal was to avoid any risky go-between. The best way to do that was to take the money straight from my pocket—without me even knowing it was there. It's genius!"

"Oh yes, genius," Moncharmin agreed, "except you're forgetting one thing, Richard. I paid for half that money—ten thousand francs— and nobody put anything in my pocket!"

Chapter XVII
The Safety-Pin Again

Moncharmin's last comment clearly showed he no longer trusted his partner, Richard. As expected, it led to a heated argument. In the end, they agreed that Richard would follow all of Moncharmin's instructions so they could finally figure out who was tricking them.

That brings us to the intermission after the Garden Scene—the same one where Remy noticed the managers acting so strangely. Richard and Moncharmin had made a plan: first, Richard would repeat everything he did on the night the twenty thousand francs disappeared. Second, Moncharmin would carefully watch Richard's coat pocket, where Madame Giry was supposed to slip the money.

Richard went to the exact place where he had stood before, the night he greeted the under-secretary for fine arts. Moncharmin stood a few steps behind him.

As planned, Madame Giry passed by, brushed against Richard, and secretly placed the envelope with the money into the tail pocket of his coat—then quickly vanished. Or rather, she was quietly taken away. Following Moncharmin's earlier instructions, Mercier brought Madame Giry to the acting manager's office and locked her inside so she couldn't contact the ghost.

Meanwhile, Richard was performing his role. He bowed, nodded, and backed up respectfully, just as he had done in front of the minister that night. Only this time, there was no one in front of him. So his odd behavior looked completely ridiculous to the others watching. He bowed to nobody, bent his back for nobody, and walked backward away from nobody. A few steps behind, Moncharmin copied him—while also pushing people aside and warning others like Remy, the ambassador, and the Credit Central manager not to touch Richard.

Moncharmin had his own reasons for doing this. He didn't want Richard coming back later and blaming someone else for the money disappearing—like the ambassador, the banker, or Remy. Especially since, as Richard himself had admitted, he hadn't seen anyone after Madame Giry brushed past him that first time.

Richard, once he began walking backward to mimic that night, kept doing so to be cautious. Moncharmin stayed close behind him, keeping him in full view, while Richard watched the front. The strange sight of the two managers creeping through the backstage area like that definitely turned heads, but they didn't care—they were focused only on the money.

When they reached a dim hallway, Richard whispered, "No one touched me. You should fall back a little now and watch me from a distance. We don't want to draw suspicion."

But Moncharmin said firmly, "No, Richard. You go ahead, and I'll stay right behind you. I won't let you out of my sight."

"If you do that," Richard complained, "then how will the money get stolen?"

"That's the point!" Moncharmin replied. "It shouldn't get stolen."

"Then this is all pointless," Richard muttered.

"No," Moncharmin said. "We're doing exactly what we did before. Remember? I met you right after you left the stage and followed you down this hallway."

"You're right," Richard sighed and continued walking, following Moncharmin's lead.

A few minutes later, both men locked themselves in the office. Moncharmin kept the key in his own pocket.

"We stayed locked in here last time too," he said, "until you left the Opera to go home."

"That's right. No one came in or bothered us, right?"

"No one," Moncharmin replied.

"Then," said Richard, trying to remember everything clearly, "the money must have been stolen on my way home from the Opera."

"No," Moncharmin said firmly. "That's not possible. I dropped you off in my cab. The money disappeared after you got home. There's no doubt about it."

"That's unbelievable!" Richard said. "I trust my servants. And if one of them had taken it, he would've run off by now."

Moncharmin just shrugged like he didn't want to argue about it anymore. Richard started feeling like Moncharmin was treating him unfairly.

"I've had enough of this!" Richard snapped.

"And I've had too much!" Moncharmin shot back.

"Are you accusing me now?"

"Yes—of playing a stupid joke."

"You don't joke around with twenty thousand francs!"

"Exactly!" Moncharmin said, opening a newspaper and pretending to read it.

"What are you doing now?" Richard asked. "Reading the paper?"

"Yes, until it's time to take you home."

"Like you did last time?"

"Exactly like last time."

Richard yanked the paper out of Moncharmin's hands. Moncharmin stood up, clearly annoyed, and saw Richard standing in front of him with his arms crossed.

"Let me tell you what I'm thinking," Richard said. "I'm thinking about what I might think if, like last time, you spend the evening with me, take me home—and once I get there, I find the money has vanished from my coat pocket again."

"And what exactly would you think?" Moncharmin asked, red with anger.

"I'd think that since you stayed right next to me all night and were the only one who came close to me, just like last time... well, if the twenty thousand francs go missing again, there's a good chance they ended up in your pocket."

Moncharmin exploded.

"Oh, really? A safety pin! Give me a safety pin!"

"What for?" Richard asked.

"To pin you to the money! That way, whether we're here or on the way to your house, you'll know exactly who's touching your coat pocket. If someone tries to take the money, you'll feel it—and you'll see it's not me! So now you're suspecting me?"

Then Moncharmin flung the office door open and yelled into the hallway, "A safety pin! Someone get me a safety pin!"

At that very moment, Remy came to the office, only to be yelled at by Moncharmin. A boy finally brought the long-awaited pin. Moncharmin locked the door again, then knelt behind Richard.

"You still have the real notes, right?" he asked.

"I think so," Richard said.

"Are they the real ones?" Moncharmin asked carefully. He didn't want to be tricked again.

"See for yourself," Richard said. "I'm not touching them."

Moncharmin reached into Richard's pocket and pulled out the envelope. His hands shook a little as he checked the money. He hadn't sealed or closed the envelope this time so he could check more easily. All the notes were still there, and they were real. He put them back carefully and used the safety pin to fasten the envelope securely inside the pocket.

Then he sat behind Richard, eyes locked on the coat-tail pocket, while Richard stayed still at his desk.

"Just a little more patience, Richard," said Moncharmin. "It's almost midnight. Last time, we left right after the clock struck twelve."

"I've got all the patience in the world," Richard replied.

The minutes dragged on—quiet, tense, and heavy. The room felt strange. Richard tried to lighten the mood with a joke.

"If this keeps up, I might start believing the ghost really can do anything," he said. "Don't you feel it? Like the air in here is... weird? Creepy? Like something's about to happen?"

"You're absolutely right," Moncharmin said, clearly shaken.

"The ghost!" Richard whispered, lowering his voice like he was afraid someone—someone invisible—might be listening. "The ghost! What if it really is a ghost that puts those strange envelopes on the table... that speaks in Box Five... that killed Joseph Buquet... that made the chandelier fall... and that keeps stealing from us? Because, look at the facts: there's nobody here but you and me. And if the money disappears, and it's not you or me, then... maybe we have to believe the ghost is real."

At that moment, the clock on the mantel clicked, warning that it was about to strike. Then came the first chime of midnight.

Both men froze. Sweat dripped down their faces. Each chime sounded louder than the last.

When the twelfth and final strike faded, they sighed in relief and stood up.

"I guess it's time to go," Moncharmin said.

"Yes, let's," Richard replied.

"Wait—do you mind if I check your pocket first?"

"Of course not, go ahead!"

Moncharmin reached for the coat-tail pocket.

"Well?" Richard asked.

"I can feel the pin," Moncharmin said slowly.

"Obviously. Like you said, if someone tried to steal the money, we'd notice right away."

But Moncharmin didn't stop feeling around. Suddenly, he shouted, "I can feel the pin—but the money's gone!"

"Stop joking around, Moncharmin! This isn't funny."

"I'm not joking! Check it yourself!"

Richard yanked off his coat, and together they turned the pocket inside out. The pocket was completely empty.

But the safety pin? Still there, right where Moncharmin had fastened it.

Both men went pale. There was no longer any explanation—other than something supernatural.

"The ghost..." Moncharmin whispered.

Then, out of nowhere, Richard lunged at him.

"You're the only one who touched my pocket! Give me back the twenty thousand francs! Hand it over!"

"I swear on my life," Moncharmin gasped, nearly fainting, "I don't have it!"

Just then, there was a knock on the door. Moncharmin opened it automatically. It was Mercier, the business manager. Moncharmin barely seemed to recognize him. He mumbled a few words without thinking, and absentmindedly handed him the safety pin—now completely useless.

Chapter XVIII
The Commissary, The Viscount and the Persian

The first thing the police officer said when he entered the managers' office was:

"Is Christine Daaé here?"

"Christine Daaé?" Richard repeated. "No, she's not. Why?"

Moncharmin was so shaken he couldn't say a word.

Richard asked again, this time for the officer and the crowd that had followed him into the office, who were now completely silent:

"Why are you asking if Christine is here, sir?"

"Because we need to find her," said the officer seriously.

"What do you mean? Has she gone missing?"

"She vanished in the middle of the show."

"In the middle of the show? That's unbelievable!"

"It is," the officer agreed. "And what's just as strange is that you had to hear it from me first!"

Richard groaned and buried his face in his hands.

"Another disaster... This is too much. I should just quit," he muttered, pulling at his mustache without even noticing.

"So she disappeared during the performance?" he asked again.

"Yes, right in the Prison Scene, when she was singing to the angels for help. But I don't think it was an angel who took her."

"I do!" said a voice.

Everyone turned. A young man stood there, pale and shaking with emotion.

"I'm sure it was," he said again.

"Sure of what?" asked Mifroid, the officer.

"That Christine Daaé was taken by an angel, sir. And I know his name."

"Oh? Vicomte de Chagny, you're saying she was taken by an angel? An angel of the Opera, I suppose?"

"Yes, exactly. And I can tell you where he lives... if we can speak in private."

"You're right, we should," the officer said.

He offered Raoul a chair and told everyone else to leave the room, except for the two managers.

Then Raoul began:

"Sir, the angel's name is Erik. He lives somewhere in the Opera House, and he's known as the Angel of Music."

"The Angel of Music? That's... quite something," the officer said. Then he turned to the managers. "Gentlemen, do you have an 'Angel of Music' working here?"

Richard and Moncharmin just shook their heads silently.

Raoul continued, "These two know about the Opera Ghost. What I'm telling you is that the ghost and the Angel of Music are the same person. His real name is Erik."

The officer stood up and looked at Raoul closely.

"Excuse me, sir, but are you trying to make fun of the law? If not, then what's this story about a ghost?"

"I'm saying they've heard of him," Raoul replied, nodding at the managers.

The officer turned to them. "Gentlemen, do you know anything about this Opera Ghost?"

Richard stood up, still holding the last few hairs of his mustache in his hand.

"No, officer, we don't know him," Richard said. "But we wish we did, because tonight he stole twenty thousand francs from us!"

He shot a threatening look at Moncharmin, clearly thinking: Give the money back or I'll spill everything.

Moncharmin got the message and threw up his hands. "Fine, just tell the whole story already."

Commissary Mifroid looked from the managers to Raoul, unsure if he'd walked into a madhouse. He ran a hand through his hair and said, "A ghost who, in one night, kidnaps a singer and steals a small fortune? That ghost must be pretty busy! But let's take one thing at a time—first the singer, then the money. Now, M. de Chagny, let's try to talk seriously. You believe Christine Daaé was taken by someone named Erik. Do you know this man? Have you ever seen him?"

"Yes," Raoul replied.

"Where?"

"In a graveyard."

The commissary blinked and looked Raoul over again. "Of course. That's where ghosts usually hang out. And what were you doing in a graveyard?"

"I understand this all sounds crazy," said Raoul. "But I promise I'm thinking clearly. Christine's life may be in danger. I don't have much time, and I need you to take me seriously. I'll tell you everything I know about the Opera ghost. Sadly, it's not much."

"Go on, go on!" Richard and Moncharmin said eagerly.

But it didn't take long for them to realize that Raoul's story—about skulls and ghostly violins in Perros-Guirec—sounded like the wild imagination of a man hopelessly in love. The commissary seemed to think the same and would probably have cut Raoul off if something unexpected hadn't happened.

The door opened, and a strange man entered. He wore a big, worn-out coat and an old, tall hat that almost covered his ears. He whispered something to the commissary, who kept watching Raoul the entire time.

Then he turned and said, "Now let's talk about you, M. de Chagny. You were planning to run away with Mlle. Daaé tonight, right?"

"Yes, sir."

"After the show?"

"Yes."

"You had everything prepared?"

"Yes."

"The carriage that brought you was supposed to take you both away, with fresh horses waiting along the route?"

"Yes, that's true."

"And yet your carriage is still parked outside, isn't it?"

"Yes, sir."

"Did you notice there were three other carriages there besides yours?"

"No, I didn't pay attention."

"They belonged to Mlle. Sorelli, Carlotta, and your brother, the Comte de Chagny."

"Okay…"

"Well, your carriage, Sorelli's, and Carlotta's are still there. But your brother's carriage is gone."

"That has nothing to do with—"

"Excuse me. Wasn't your brother against your relationship with Christine?"

"That's a family matter."

"But you've just answered my question. He was against it, and that's why you planned to take Christine away from him. But, M. de Chagny, let me tell you—your brother outsmarted you. He's the one who took Christine Daaé!"

"No… that's not possible!" Raoul gasped, clutching his chest. "Are you sure?"

"Right after she disappeared during the show, he rushed her into his carriage, which took off through the streets of Paris at top speed."

"Through Paris?" Raoul said weakly. "What do you mean, through Paris?"

"I mean they left the city. The carriage took the road toward Brussels."

"I'll catch them!" Raoul cried and ran from the room.

"Bring her back!" the commissary called after him, laughing. "Now that's how you outsmart a ghost!"

Turning to the group, Mifroid began a little speech.

"Now, I can't say for certain whether the Count really did kidnap Mlle. Daaé, but one thing's clear: nobody wants to find out the truth more than Raoul. And now he's chasing after his brother for us. That, gentlemen, is the art of police work. People think it's complicated, but often it's just getting others to do the job for you."

But M. Mifroid wouldn't have been so proud of himself if he had known what happened next. As soon as Raoul tried to leave the building, someone blocked his path.

A tall man stood in front of him and said, "Where are you rushing off to, M. de Chagny?"

Raoul looked up quickly and saw the familiar fur hat.

"It's you!" he cried. "The one who warned me not to speak Erik's name! Who are you?"

"You know who I am," the man replied calmly. "I'm the Persian."

Chapter XIX
The Viscount and the Persian

Raoul suddenly remembered that his brother had once pointed out this mysterious man to him—the man known only as "the Persian." No one knew much about him, except that he lived alone in a small, old-fashioned apartment on Rue de Rivoli.

The man, with his dark skin, bright greenish eyes, and fur-lined hat, leaned closer to Raoul.

"I hope you haven't revealed Erik's secret, M. de Chagny," he said quietly.

"And why wouldn't I?" Raoul replied sharply, trying to brush past him. "Is he your friend?"

"I only ask because Erik's secret is also Christine Daaé's. If you speak of one, you reveal the other."

"Sir," Raoul said impatiently, "you clearly know things that matter to me—but I don't have time to talk. I need to help Christine!"

"Then don't go anywhere," the Persian said calmly, "because Christine is here."

"She's here? With Erik?"

"Yes."

"How do you know that?"

"I was at the performance tonight. No one else but Erik could have pulled off something like that. I could tell—it had his mark all over it."

"So you do know him?"

The Persian didn't answer. He just let out a deep sigh.

"Sir," Raoul said, trying to stay calm, "I don't know what you want, but can you help me save Christine?"

"I believe I can, M. de Chagny. That's why I stopped you."

"What can you do?"

"I can try to take you to her... and to him."

"If you can do that, I owe you my life! But one more thing—the police say that my brother, Count Philippe, is the one who took Christine."

The Persian shook his head. "I don't believe that for a second."

"It doesn't seem possible, does it?"

"I can't say for sure, but let's be honest—there are many ways to kidnap someone, and I don't think your brother has ever been known to use magic."

"You're right... I've been an idiot. Please—let's hurry. I'm putting my full trust in you. How could I not, when you're the only one who believes me? The only one who doesn't laugh when I mention Erik?"

Raoul grabbed the Persian's hands in a rush of emotion. They were ice-cold.

"Quiet!" the Persian whispered. He stopped and listened to faint sounds coming from deeper in the building. "We must not say his name here. Let's call him 'he' or 'him.' That way we're less likely to attract his attention."

"You think he might be close?"

"It's possible. If he's not with Christine right now—in the house by the lake—he could be here. In these walls... in the floor... or even in the ceiling."

"Wait, you know about the house on the lake too?"

The Persian nodded. "Come. Be quiet. Step softly."

He led Raoul through a series of hidden hallways Raoul had never seen before, not even when Christine used to take him exploring behind the scenes.

"I hope Darius has come," the Persian muttered.

"Who's Darius?"

"My servant."

They entered a large, empty space dimly lit by a single lamp. The room felt like a forgotten square buried deep in the Opera House. The Persian stopped and whispered, "What did you tell the commissary?"

"I said Christine was taken by the Angel of Music—also known as the Opera Ghost. I told him the ghost's real name was—"

"Shh!" the Persian hissed. "And did he believe you?"

"No."

"He didn't think it mattered?"

"No."

"He thought you were crazy?"

"Yes."

"Good," the Persian breathed, almost in relief.

They kept walking, moving through stairways Raoul had never seen before. Finally, they stopped in front of a door, which the Persian unlocked with a master key. Both men were dressed in formal clothes, but while Raoul wore a tall top hat, the Persian had on his usual fur-lined astrakhan cap. Normally, top hats were required backstage, but since the Persian was a foreigner, exceptions were made—just like they were for English visitors and their traveling caps.

"Your hat will only get in the way," said the Persian. "You should leave it in the dressing room."

"Which dressing room?" Raoul asked.

"Christine Daaé's."

The Persian led Raoul through the door and pointed to a room across the hall. They were now at the end of the same hallway Raoul used to walk down when visiting Christine.

"You know this place well," Raoul said.

"Not as well as he does," the Persian answered quietly.

He guided Raoul into Christine's room, which looked just as it had earlier. Then the Persian walked over to a thin wall between the dressing room and a large storage room. He listened closely, then gave a loud cough. A moment later, there was a soft knock at the door.

"Come in," said the Persian.

Another man entered, wearing a long coat and an astrakhan cap like the Persian's. He bowed, pulled a finely carved case from under his coat, placed it on the dressing table, bowed again, and turned to leave.

"Did anyone see you come in, Darius?" the Persian asked.

"No, sir."

"Make sure no one sees you leave, either."

Darius looked down the hallway and slipped out quickly.

The Persian opened the case. Inside was a pair of long pistols.

"When Christine was taken, I sent for these," he explained. "They're old, but very dependable."

"You're planning to fight a duel?" Raoul asked.

"It will be a duel, yes," the Persian replied, checking the guns. "And not just any duel—we're going up against a terrifying enemy. But you love Christine Daaé, don't you?"

"I'd give my life for her!" Raoul answered. "But you—you don't love her. So why would you risk your life for her? You must hate Erik!"

"No," said the Persian sadly, "I don't hate him. If I did, he would've stopped hurting people long ago."

"Has he hurt you before?"

"I've forgiven him for what he did to me."

"I don't understand. You say he's a monster, a criminal, and still you pity him. Christine pitied him, too, and it drove me crazy."

The Persian didn't answer. Instead, he brought over a stool and placed it in front of the large mirror covering the wall. Climbing onto the stool, he leaned close to the wallpaper and searched for something with his nose nearly touching the wall.

"Ah, here it is!" he said after a moment.

He pressed a small spot hidden in the wallpaper pattern. Then he climbed down and crossed the room to the mirror.

"In about thirty seconds," he said, "it'll be ready."

He pressed his hands against the mirror.

"No, not just yet," he muttered.

"We're going out through the mirror?" Raoul asked. "Like Christine?"

"So you saw her disappear through it?"

"Yes. I was hiding in the other room and saw her vanish—not behind the mirror, but into it."

"What did you do?"

"I thought I was imagining things. I thought I was going crazy."

"Or maybe it's another one of the ghost's tricks!" the Persian said with a strange chuckle. Then, keeping one hand on the mirror, he added, "Oh, M. de Chagny, if only we really were dealing with a ghost! Then we could leave our pistols where they are. But this is something else… Now please, set down your hat—there—and try to hide your white shirtfront as much as you can. Do what I'm doing. Pull your coat closed, bring the lapels in, and turn up your collar. We have to make ourselves as hard to see as possible."

After a short pause, still pressing against the mirror, he said, "It takes time to release the counterweight when you're pressing the hidden spring from inside the room. It's much easier from the other side, where you can act on the mechanism directly. Then the mirror spins quickly and smoothly."

"Counterweight?" Raoul asked.

"Yes, the balance that lifts this entire wall and puts it on a pivot. You didn't think it moves by magic, did you? Watch closely—you'll see the mirror rise a little, shift to one side, and then swing around."

"It's not moving!" Raoul said impatiently.

"Be patient! The mechanism might be rusty, or maybe the spring isn't catching... unless..." The Persian's tone changed, sounding worried.

"Unless what?"

"He might have cut the cord that operates the counterweight. He could have blocked the whole system."

"But why would he do that? He doesn't know we're trying to get in this way!"

"Maybe not—but he probably suspects it. He knows I understand how this passage works."

"It's still not turning... And Christine—what about Christine?"

The Persian spoke calmly, but seriously. "We'll do everything we can... but he might stop us before we even get started. He controls the walls, the doors, and the trapdoors. Back in my country, he had a name that meant 'the master of trapdoors.'"

"But why do these walls only obey him? He didn't build the Opera House!"

"That's just it," the Persian said. "He did."

Raoul stared at him, stunned. But the Persian quickly motioned for silence and pointed at the mirror. There was a strange shimmer in the glass—like the surface of water being disturbed. Their reflection rippled and then went still again.

"You see? It's not moving! Let's find another way in!"

"Tonight, there is no other way," the Persian replied with a heavy tone. "Now be careful. Be ready to shoot if you have to."

He lifted his pistol and aimed it at the mirror. Raoul copied him. With his free hand, the Persian pulled Raoul close, and then suddenly, the mirror spun around like a revolving door. Lights flashed and blurred around them. In an instant, they were pulled from the brightly lit dressing room into complete darkness.

Chapter XX
In the Cellars of the Opera

"Keep your hand up—be ready to shoot!" Raoul's guide whispered urgently.

Behind them, the wall they had come through slowly spun back into place, sealing them off in total darkness. The two men stood still, holding their breath.

After a moment, the Persian knelt down and began feeling along the floor with his hands. Then a small red light flicked on, casting a soft glow through the darkness. Raoul stepped back at first, thinking someone else had found them. But it was just the Persian using a small dark lantern to look around. Raoul watched closely as the light moved over the wooden floor, walls, and ceiling. Everything around them was made of planks, like a secret tunnel.

Raoul remembered the Persian saying that Erik had built this hidden passage to reach Christine's dressing room without being seen. Later, Raoul would learn that Erik hadn't built it himself—it had already been there for years. It was a leftover from the time of the Paris Commune. The government had once used this tunnel to secretly move prisoners down to jail cells built in the Opera's cellars. The rebels had even turned the roof into a launch pad for hot-air balloons, which carried their messages across France.

The Persian set the lantern on the ground and started working on something at the floor. Suddenly, he turned off the light. A moment later, there was a quiet click, and a soft white glow appeared in the floor, as if a small window had opened to the level below. Raoul couldn't see the Persian anymore, but he felt him draw close and whisper in his ear:

"Do exactly as I do."

Raoul turned toward the opening in the floor. He saw the Persian, still kneeling, grab the edges of the hole with both hands, grip his pistol between his teeth, and quietly slide down through the trapdoor into the cellar below.

Even though Raoul barely knew the man, he completely trusted him. The Persian's emotion when talking about Erik seemed genuine. And if he had meant Raoul harm, he wouldn't have given him a weapon. Raoul had to get to Christine, no matter what. So, he followed the Persian's lead. He grabbed the edge of the trap with both hands.

"Let go," the Persian whispered.

Raoul released his grip and dropped—straight into the Persian's waiting arms. The man quickly told him to lie flat, then shut the trapdoor and crouched beside him.

Raoul tried to speak, but the Persian clamped a hand over his mouth. Then Raoul heard a voice he recognized—it was the police commissary.

The two men were hidden behind a wooden wall. Not far from them, a small staircase led to a nearby room where the commissary was pacing, asking questions. The dim light was just enough for Raoul to make out his surroundings. What he saw made him gasp softly: three dead bodies lay nearby.

One was sprawled across the landing at the top of the stairs. The other two were at the bottom. Raoul was so close to one of them, he could have reached out and touched it through a gap in the wood.

"Quiet," the Persian whispered.

He had seen the bodies too, and he gave one chilling explanation:

"Him."

They listened quietly as the commissary's voice became clearer. He was asking about how the lighting system worked, and the stage manager was explaining it to him. That meant the commissary was now standing in or near the "organ."

In an opera house, the "organ" wasn't a musical instrument. Back then, electricity was used only for a few special effects and some bells. Most of the lighting came from gas. A special setup called the "organ," filled with pipes, controlled the gas lights and could change how scenes looked onstage. It was operated from a small room next to the prompter's box, where the head gas-man, Mauclair, would stay during every performance to make sure everything ran smoothly.

Now Mauclair wasn't in his control booth, and none of his assistants were in their usual spots either.

"Mauclair! Mauclair!"

The stage manager's voice echoed through the basement. But there was no answer.

Earlier, a door had been spotted near a small staircase leading down to a lower level. The commissary tried to open it, but it wouldn't budge.

"This door won't open," he said to the stage manager. "Is it always this hard?"

The stage manager shoved it open with his shoulder—and gasped. He had pushed against a body.

"It's Mauclair! Poor guy… He's dead!"

But the commissary, who was not easily shocked, leaned down to check.

"No, he's not dead," he said calmly. "He's just passed out—completely drunk. That's not the same thing."

"That's strange. I've never seen him like this before," said the stage manager.

"Someone may have drugged him," Mifroid suggested. "It's definitely possible."

He stepped down a few more stairs and called back, "Look!"

By the glow of a small red lantern, they saw two more bodies at the bottom of the stairs. The stage manager quickly recognized them as Mauclair's assistants. Mifroid bent over and checked their breathing.

"They're just asleep," he said. "This is very strange. Someone must have taken them out of the way—and clearly it was someone working for whoever kidnapped the girl. But who kidnaps someone right off the stage during a show?"

He turned to an assistant. "Send for the theater doctor."

Then he repeated to himself, "This is definitely a strange case…"

Turning back toward a small room, he called out to some people Raoul and the Persian couldn't see from where they were hiding:

"Well, gentlemen? You two haven't said anything yet. Surely you must have some kind of opinion about all this."

Raoul and the Persian then saw the surprised faces of the two theater managers peeking over the landing. Moncharmin's nervous voice answered:

"Something is going on here, Mr. Commissary, but we don't understand any of it."

And with that, the managers vanished from sight again.

"Thanks for clearing that up," Mifroid said sarcastically.

Meanwhile, the stage manager was standing in deep thought, with his chin resting in his hand.

"This isn't the first time Mauclair has fallen asleep in the theater," he said slowly. "I once found him dozing in his little corner, snuff-box beside him."

"Was that long ago?" asked Mifroid as he cleaned his glasses.

"No, not really… Wait a second! Yes—of course—it was the same night that Carlotta croaked onstage. Remember? That famous 'co-ack' moment?"

"Ah yes," said Mifroid, now putting his glasses back on. He stared thoughtfully at the stage manager.

"So Mauclair takes snuff, does he?" he asked casually.

"Yes, sir. See his snuff-box over there on the shelf? He uses it all the time."

"So do I," said Mifroid—and he slipped the snuff-box into his pocket.

Hidden and unnoticed, Raoul and the Persian quietly watched as workers came to carry away the three unconscious men. The commissary and his team followed them upstairs, and for a few minutes, their footsteps echoed faintly above.

When the coast was clear, the Persian motioned for Raoul to stand. He got up, but lowered his gun. The Persian stopped him immediately.

"Keep your hand up and be ready to shoot—no matter what," he whispered.

"But my arm's getting tired," Raoul whispered back. "If I need to shoot, I won't be able to aim properly."

"Then switch hands," the Persian replied.

"I can't shoot with my left hand," Raoul said.

The Persian gave a strange reply that didn't exactly help calm Raoul's nerves.

"It's not really about which hand you use. What matters is keeping one of your arms bent like you're ready to fire, as if holding a gun. You can actually keep the pistol in your pocket." Then he added, "Understand this clearly—or I won't be responsible for what happens. This is life or death. Now be quiet and follow me."

The Opera's cellars were massive, five levels deep. Raoul followed the Persian, wondering how he would have ever found his way without him in such a maze. They descended to the third basement, still guided by a few dim lights in the distance.

The deeper they went, the more careful the Persian became. He kept glancing back to make sure Raoul held his arm correctly—raised and bent like he was ready to draw and shoot, even though his pistol stayed tucked in his pocket.

Suddenly, a loud voice echoed from above:

"Close all the doors on stage! The police commissary needs them closed!"

They heard footsteps and saw shadows moving in the dark. The Persian quickly pulled Raoul behind a large stage prop. From there, they saw a group of elderly men shuffling past. Some could barely move; others felt their way around by habit, looking for doors to shut.

These were the "door-shutters," old stagehands the Opera had kept on out of kindness. Their job was to close doors all around the theater to keep drafts out, which could damage singers' voices. Many of them had nowhere else to go, so they stayed in the Opera overnight.

Raoul and the Persian were lucky—the police inspection meant these men wouldn't be lying around where they might trip over them and ask questions.

But their quiet didn't last. More figures began coming down the same way. These new people each held a small lantern, sweeping the light up and down, side to side, as if searching for someone—or something.

"Damn," the Persian muttered. "I don't know what they're looking for, but they could easily spot us. We've got to move—quick!"

"Raise your hand like I showed you, ready to fire! Bend your arm... yes, higher... like you're waiting for someone to shout 'Fire!' Don't take the pistol out, leave it in your pocket! Let's go! Down these stairs—your hand up! Remember, it's life or death!"

They rushed down to the fifth cellar. Once there, the Persian finally stopped to catch his breath. He seemed slightly more at ease, but still held his arm in the same strange position. Raoul thought again about what the Persian had said earlier: "These pistols are reliable." But it made no sense—why rely on weapons if they weren't going to use them?

The Persian didn't give Raoul time to think. He told him to stay put, ran back up a few steps to peek around, then returned.

"How foolish of us," he whispered. "Those people with the lanterns? They were just the firemen making their rounds."

They waited quietly for another five minutes. Then the Persian led Raoul back up the stairs. But just as they began climbing, he suddenly raised a hand and stopped him.

"Get down—flat on the floor!" he whispered sharply.

They dropped just in time. A dark shape passed by—no lantern this time. Just a shadow moving in deeper shadow, gliding so close it nearly brushed against them.

They could feel the warmth of the cloak brushing against them as it passed. They could see just enough to tell that the figure was completely wrapped in a cloak from head to toe. It wore a soft felt hat pulled low over its head.

The figure moved away slowly, sliding its feet along the wall and sometimes kicking into corners.

"Whew!" whispered the Persian. "That was close. That shadow knows who I am—it's taken me to the managers' office twice before."

"Is it someone from the theater police?" Raoul asked.

"No," said the Persian quietly, "it's someone far more dangerous." He didn't explain any further.

"It's not... him, is it?"

"If he comes from in front, we'll see his glowing yellow eyes. That's our only real protection tonight. But if he sneaks up from behind, we won't see him—and we're dead men if we're not ready. Keep your hand up like you're going to fire—at eye level!"

The Persian had barely finished speaking when something terrifying appeared: a glowing face, not just eyes—a whole face of fire. It floated toward them, about the height of a man's head, but with no body attached. It glowed like a flame shaped like a human face.

"Oh no," the Persian muttered through clenched teeth. "I've never seen this before! Pampin wasn't crazy—he really did see it! What is that? It's not him, but maybe he sent it. Be careful! Be careful! Keep your hand at eye level! I know many of his tricks, but not this one. Run— it's safer! Keep your hand up!"

They turned and ran down a dark hallway.

Seconds passed like minutes. Finally, they stopped to catch their breath.

"He doesn't usually come this way," said the Persian. "This side doesn't lead to the lake or the house on the lake. But maybe he knows we're following him... even though I promised never to interfere with his business again."

They both looked back—and there it was. The fiery face had followed them. It must have moved faster than they had, because it seemed even closer now.

At the same time, they started hearing a strange sound that they couldn't quite place. It grew louder as the face came closer. It sounded like thousands of nails scratching across a chalkboard, that terrible, screeching noise made when a small stone gets caught in a piece of chalk.

They kept backing away, but the face came closer and closer. Now they could see its features clearly—round, wide eyes, a crooked nose, and a large mouth with a drooping lower lip. It looked like the red, glowing face of the moon.

But how was this floating, fiery face moving through the air with nothing holding it up? And how did it move so fast, so directly, with those strange, staring eyes? And what was that awful scratching sound following it?

Raoul and the Persian couldn't go any farther. They pressed themselves against the wall, completely frozen with fear. The scratching sound had become something more—it was a buzzing, crawling sound, like hundreds of tiny things scurrying through the dark. It was no longer one sound, but a swarm of little noises moving just beneath the floating face.

And then the face reached them.

They were terrified. Their hair stood on end. Now they knew what those hundreds of tiny sounds were. Something rushed at them like waves crashing on the shore, brushing against their legs and climbing up. Raoul and the Persian couldn't help crying out in horror and pain. They dropped their arms to try and push away whatever was crawling on them.

The swarm was full of tiny legs, sharp claws, teeth, and nails. They were rats—hundreds of them, maybe thousands.

Just when they thought they would pass out from the fear and the pain, the glowing face turned toward them and spoke:

"Don't move! Stay where you are! Whatever you do, don't follow me! I'm the rat-catcher! Let me through with my rats!"

Then the face vanished into the darkness, and the path ahead lit up as the man turned his lantern forward. He had been pointing it at himself to keep from scaring the rats—so that's why only his head had been glowing. Now he lit the way forward to keep the rats moving ahead.

He leapt ahead through the hallway, followed by the rustling, scratching wave of rats.

Raoul and the Persian could finally breathe again, though they were still shaking from the terrifying encounter.

"I should've remembered that Erik once told me about the rat-catcher," said the Persian. "But he never mentioned what he looked like. Strange that I've never seen him before... Then again, Erik never comes down this far."

"Are we close to the lake?" Raoul asked. "When will we get there? Please, take me to the lake! Once we're there, we can call out—Christine will hear us! And so will he! Since you know him, maybe we can talk to him!"

"You're being foolish," said the Persian. "We're not going to reach the house by crossing the lake. I've never even reached the shore where the house stands. You have to go across first, and it's well guarded. I'm afraid more than a few people—old workers and door-shutters—tried to cross and were never seen again. It's dangerous. I almost died there once myself... if Erik hadn't recognized me just in time."

He lowered his voice.

"Here's some advice: never go near the lake. And above all, if you hear singing from under the water—a voice like a siren—don't listen."

"Then why are we even here?" Raoul burst out, his voice filled with frustration and desperation. "If you can't help Christine, at least let me die trying to save her!"

The Persian tried to calm him. "We have only one hope of saving her. And that's to sneak into the house without Erik knowing."

"Is that even possible?" Raoul asked.

"If I didn't believe it was, I wouldn't have come to find you," the Persian said. "And we can get there without crossing the lake."

"How?"

"Through the third cellar, the one we had to leave earlier. We're going back there now. I'll show you the exact spot. It's between a set piece and an old backdrop from Roi de Lahore, right where Joseph Buquet died. Be brave and follow me. Keep your hand up by your eyes—just like I showed you. Wait... where are we?"

The Persian turned on his lamp and shined it down two long hallways that crossed each other.

"We're in the section used mostly for the waterworks," he said. "I don't see any fire from the furnaces."

He walked ahead, carefully checking the way and freezing every time he feared they might run into someone. Once, they had to hide from the glow of an underground forge, where some workers were putting out the fire. Raoul recognized them—they looked like the strange men Christine had seen when she was first taken.

Step by step, they made their way down to the deepest cellars under the stage. They were now at the bottom of what was known as "the tub," buried far below the water that lay beneath that whole area of Paris.

The Persian knocked gently on a wall. "If I'm right, this wall is part of the lake house."

He had tapped one of the inner walls of the massive foundation built to keep water away from the opera's machinery. To anyone who knew the building well, his gesture made it clear: Erik's hidden house had to be built inside the thick double wall. This wall had been created to act like a dam, made of brick and cement, layer after layer, several yards thick.

Raoul pressed his ear to the wall, listening as hard as he could, but heard nothing—just distant footsteps far above.

The Persian turned off the lamp again.

"Be careful," he whispered. "Keep your hand raised. Stay silent. We'll try another way in."

He led Raoul back to the narrow staircase they'd taken before. Slowly, step by step, stopping often, they made their way back to the third cellar. Once there, the Persian signaled for Raoul to drop to his knees. Crawling on both knees and one hand—since the other still had to be held up—they reached the back wall.

A large, discarded piece of scenery from Roi de Lahore leaned against it. Next to it stood a set piece. Between the two was just enough space for one body.

The same spot where Joseph Buquet had once been found hanging.

Still kneeling, the Persian stopped and listened carefully. He glanced up toward the second cellar, where a dim light was shining through a narrow gap between two wooden boards. The glow seemed to make him uneasy. After thinking for a moment, he gave a quick nod, like he had made a decision, and then crawled forward between the large prop and the old backdrop from Roi de Lahore, with Raoul following closely behind.

The Persian ran his hand along the wall, just like he had in Christine's dressing room. Then, one of the stones shifted, revealing a small opening. He took out his pistol and motioned for Raoul to do the same. They both cocked their pistols, and the Persian slid through the hole on his knees. Raoul had wanted to go first, but there wasn't room, so he followed after.

The space was tight, and they didn't get far before the Persian stopped. Raoul heard him searching the stones, then saw him light his small lantern. He bent down, looked at something carefully, and then quickly turned the light off.

"We'll have to drop down a few feet without making noise," the Persian whispered. "Take off your boots."

He handed Raoul his own shoes. "Leave them outside the wall. We'll pick them up later."

He crawled ahead a little, turned around, and said, "I'm going to hang by my hands and drop into his house. Do exactly as I do. Don't be scared. I'll catch you."

Raoul soon heard the soft thud of the Persian landing and then dropped down himself. The Persian caught him as promised.

"Quiet," he said.

They stood still, surrounded by deep darkness and heavy silence.

Then the Persian turned on the lantern again and searched the floor and walls. He looked for the opening they had come through—but it had vanished.

"Oh no," he whispered. "The stone closed by itself."

The light of the lantern moved along the floor, where the Persian bent to pick up something—a piece of rope. After examining it briefly, he threw it away with a shiver.

"The Punjab lasso," he muttered.

"What's that?" Raoul asked.

"It might be the same rope that was used to hang that poor man— Joseph Buquet. They searched for it for a long time."

Suddenly anxious, the Persian searched the walls with the lantern. The beam landed on something strange—a tree trunk with branches and leaves that climbed the walls and disappeared into the ceiling.

At first, the small beam of light made it hard to see what it really was. They could only make out parts—a branch here, a leaf there— and then nothing, only a strange reflection.

Raoul reached out and touched it.

"It's a mirror!" he said.

"Yes," the Persian said in a serious tone. "A mirror. We've fallen into the torture chamber."

What happened to them next was written down by the Persian himself in a letter, which I will now share word for word.

Chapter XXI
Interesting and Instructive Vicissitudes of a Persian in the Cellars of the Opera

THE PERSIAN'S NARRATIVE

It was my first time entering the house by the lake. I had often begged Erik—whom we called the "trap-door lover" back in my country—to let me inside. But he always refused. I tried many times to figure out how to get in, but I never had any luck. No matter how closely I watched him after learning he lived in the Opera, it was always too dark to see how he opened the secret door in the wall by the lake.

One day, thinking I was alone, I got into the boat and rowed toward the part of the wall where I'd seen Erik vanish. That's when I had a run-in with the "siren" that guarded the way—and it almost cost me my life.

As soon as I pushed off from shore, the silence was broken by a soft, whispering song. It sounded like a mix of breath and music, floating around me from all sides. It seemed to come from the water itself. It followed me and moved as I moved, but it was so gentle that it didn't scare me. Instead, I was drawn to it. I leaned over the edge of the boat, trying to get closer to the sound. I was certain the singing was coming from below the surface.

Now I was alone in the middle of the lake. The voice, now clearly a voice, seemed to be right beside me. The water was calm and dark, like ink, and moonlight from the Rue Scribe shone faintly on it—but I couldn't see anything. I even shook my head, thinking the sound might be in my ears, but it wasn't. It was real. The quiet singing pulled me in.

If I were superstitious, I might've thought it was a real siren trying to lure me to my doom. But I come from a place where we love magical stories, so I know how to see through them. I was sure this was one of Erik's inventions. Still, the trick was so good that instead of figuring out how it worked, I just wanted to enjoy the beautiful sound. I kept leaning over... more and more... until I nearly tipped the boat over.

Suddenly, two huge arms reached out of the water and grabbed me by the neck. They pulled me under so fast and hard that I couldn't fight back. I would've drowned—if I hadn't had time to shout. Erik heard my cry and recognized me. Instead of killing me, which I think he had planned to do, he swam to shore with me and gently placed me on the bank.

"You're so reckless," he said, standing over me, soaking wet. "Why did you try to get into my home? I never invited you! I don't want you—or anyone—there! You saved my life once, but that doesn't mean you can follow me around! Erik may be grateful, but even he can forget. And you know nothing can stop Erik—not even Erik himself."

He talked, but I was only thinking about the siren and how it worked. Erik gave in and told me. For all his cruelty, Erik could be childish—vain and proud of his cleverness. He loved showing off his inventions.

Laughing, he pulled out a long, hollow reed.

"It's the simplest trick," he said, "but very useful for breathing and singing underwater. I learned it from pirates in Tonkin. They use it to hide for hours under riverbeds."

I scolded him.

"That 'trick' almost killed me! And who knows who else it's harmed? You promised me—no more killing!"

"Have I really killed anyone?" he asked with a smile, trying to act innocent.

"Terrible man!" I shouted. "Have you forgotten the happy days in Mazenderan?"

His expression turned sad. "Yes," he said softly, "I try to forget them. But I did make the little sultana laugh, didn't I?"

"All that's in the past now," I told him. "But what matters is the present—and you're responsible for that. If I hadn't saved your life, Erik, you wouldn't even have a present to speak of. Don't forget that."

Then I took the chance to ask him something that had been bothering me for a while.

"Erik," I said, "swear to me that—"

"What?" he cut in. "You know I don't keep promises. Promises are just tricks to fool fools."

"Just tell me something, then. At least tell me the truth…"

"What is it?"

"The chandelier, Erik. Tell me the truth about the chandelier."

He gave a creepy little laugh. "Oh, that? I don't mind telling you. I didn't do it! That chandelier was old and ready to fall anyway."

When Erik laughed, it was terrifying. He jumped into his boat, chuckling in a way that made me shake with fear.

"Very old, my dear daroga! So old and shaky, it just crashed down on its own! And now, listen to me—go dry off or you'll catch a cold. And don't ever get in my boat again. Don't try to get into my house either. I'm not always there, and I'd hate to have to dedicate my Requiem Mass to you!"

Still laughing like a madman, he pushed off in the boat and vanished into the lake's darkness.

From that day on, I gave up trying to get into his house by the lake. That way was clearly too well guarded—especially now that Erik knew I had discovered it. But I was sure there was another way. I'd seen Erik vanish into the third cellar more than once, even though I never figured out how.

Ever since I learned he was living inside the Opera, I had lived in constant fear—not for myself, but for everyone else. Whenever something bad happened—some strange accident or disaster—I couldn't help thinking, "That must have been Erik." Others would say, "It's the ghost!" and laugh. Poor fools. If they'd known the ghost was real and alive, they would never have joked about it.

Erik once told me, very seriously, that he had changed. He said he'd become a good man now—ever since someone loved him for who he was. At first, I didn't know what to make of that. But even so, I still felt nervous just thinking about him. His terrible, unnatural appearance made him feel like he wasn't part of the human race. And I think he felt the same way. It was like he didn't believe he had any responsibility toward people. The way he spoke about love only made me more worried. I feared it would lead to something even more tragic and awful.

Later, I learned about the strange connection between Erik and Christine Daaé. I hid in a storage room near her dressing room and heard beautiful music—so incredible it made her sound amazed and joyful. Still, I didn't understand how Erik's voice—loud like thunder or soft like an angel's—could make her forget how he looked. Then I found out that she hadn't seen him yet.

One day, I had a reason to visit her dressing room. I remembered some tricks Erik had once shown me and figured out how the mirror wall could move. I found out how he used hollow bricks and secret openings to make it sound like his voice was right beside Christine, even when he was somewhere else. I also discovered the passage to the well and the old dungeon built during the time of the Communists. I found the trapdoor Erik used to get to the cellars beneath the stage.

A few days later, I was shocked to see—clearly—that Erik and Christine had finally met. I saw him leaning over a small well, sprinkling water on Christine's forehead after she had fainted. A white horse—the one from The Prophet, which had gone missing from the stables—stood calmly beside them.

I stepped out to show myself.

It was awful.

Erik's yellow eyes flared like sparks—and before I could say anything, he struck me on the head and everything went black.

When I woke up, Erik, Christine, and the white horse were gone. I was sure that poor Christine was now trapped in the house by the lake. I didn't hesitate—I decided to return to the shore, even though it was risky. I waited there for a full day, convinced that Erik would eventually need to leave to get food or supplies.

You should know, when Erik went out into public, he wore a fake nose made of cardboard with a mustache attached, to cover the awful hole where his nose should be. It didn't completely hide his creepy, corpse-like appearance, but it made him look just bearable enough that people didn't scream.

I waited by the lake for hours, starting to think that maybe he had used the other secret exit in the third cellar. But then I heard a quiet splash and saw two glowing yellow eyes—like candles—approaching. Erik's boat touched the shore. He jumped out and came straight up to me.

"You've been here for 24 hours," he said, clearly annoyed. "You're getting on my nerves. This won't end well, and it'll be your fault. I've been more than patient with you. You think you're watching me, but actually, I've been watching you. I know everything you know about me. I let you go yesterday in the old Communists' path, but don't let me catch you there again. You just don't get the message!"

He was so angry that I stayed quiet. He puffed and growled like an angry animal and continued:

"You really need to learn to back off! With the way you keep snooping around—getting caught by the man in the felt hat and being dragged to the managers—they're going to start wondering what you're up to. And when they find out you're after me, they'll come looking. If they find my house, it'll be bad for everyone. I'm warning you now: if Erik's secrets are no longer secret, it won't just be bad for me—it'll be bad for a lot of people."

He huffed again and said, "That's all I'm going to say. If you've got any sense, that'll be enough. But I know you—you never take a hint."

He sat on the edge of the boat, swinging his legs and waiting for my reply. I calmly said, "I'm not here for you, Erik."

"Then who?" he snapped.

"You already know—Christine Daaé," I answered.

"I have every right to see her in my own home," he said. "She loves me for who I am."

"That's not true," I said firmly. "You kidnapped her. You're keeping her prisoner."

"Listen," he replied. "If I can prove to you that she really loves me, will you promise to stay out of my business forever?"

"Yes," I said without hesitation. I didn't believe for a second that such a monster could be truly loved.

"Alright then," he said. "It's simple. Christine will leave this place whenever she wants—and she'll come back on her own, because she loves me. You'll see—she'll return because she wants to."

"I doubt that," I said. "But even if she does love you, it's still your responsibility to let her go."

"My duty?" he scoffed. "No, it's my wish to let her go. And she will come back, because she loves me. We're going to be married. A wedding at the Church of the Madeleine, you fool! Don't believe me? I've already written the music for the ceremony. Just wait until you hear the Kyrie!"

He banged his heels on the boat and sang: "KYRIE! KYRIE ELEISON! Wait till you hear that mass!"

"Alright," I said. "I'll believe you—if I see Christine walk out of your house and return on her own, without being forced."

"And if that happens, you'll leave me alone for good?"

"Yes," I said.

"Fine, then," Erik replied. "Tonight, go to the masquerade ball. Christine and I will take a little stroll. Hide in the lumber room and you'll see her go to her dressing room—and later return, all on her own, through the Communists' path. Now, get out of here. I've got some shopping to do!"

To my surprise, everything happened just like Erik said it would. Christine Daaé came and went from the house on the lake several times, and it didn't look like she was being forced. Even though I found it hard to stop thinking about Erik, I knew I had to be very careful. I avoided going back to the edge of the lake or using the passageway known as the Communists' road. Still, I couldn't stop thinking about the secret entrance in the third cellar. I kept going back there and waiting behind an old scene from Roi de Lahore that had been left there for some reason.

Eventually, my patience paid off. One day, I saw Erik crawling toward the wall on his knees. I was sure he didn't see me. He moved between the set piece and the old scene, pressed something on the wall, and a stone shifted, opening a hole. He slipped inside, and the stone closed behind him.

I waited half an hour, then tried pressing the same spot. Just like before, the stone moved, and the hole appeared. But I didn't go in. I knew Erik was inside, and the thought of being caught made me remember what happened to Joseph Buquet. I didn't want to risk such an important discovery, one that could help many people—as Erik himself once said, "a goodly number of the human race." So I quietly put the stone back and left the cellars.

I stayed very interested in the strange relationship between Erik and Christine—not because I was nosy, but because I was terrified of what Erik might do if he found out she didn't love him the way he believed. I kept watching from a distance, carefully. I soon discovered the truth: Christine was scared of Erik, but her heart belonged to Vicomte Raoul de Chagny. The two of them spent time together in secret on the upper floors of the Opera, unaware that someone was watching them. I was ready to protect them—if needed, even kill the monster and explain it all to the police afterward. But Erik never showed himself, which didn't make me feel any safer.

Let me explain my plan. I believed Erik might leave his house out of jealousy, giving me a chance to go in through the third cellar without being noticed. I had to find out what was inside for everyone's safety. One day, tired of waiting, I moved the stone and was stunned to hear powerful music coming from within. Erik was working on Don Juan Triumphant, his life's masterpiece, and had left all the doors in his house open. I stayed hidden and didn't move.

He stopped playing and began pacing like a madman, shouting, "It must be finished FIRST! Completely finished!" His words didn't calm me. I slowly closed the stone and backed away.

On the day Christine was taken, I didn't arrive at the Opera until late in the evening, worried about what I might hear. I had spent the whole day uneasy because I read a newspaper report announcing her engagement to Raoul. I wondered whether I should finally expose Erik to the authorities—but reason told me that would only make things worse.

When I arrived, I was surprised the Opera House was still standing. But being somewhat of a fatalist, I entered, prepared for anything. When Christine vanished during the Prison Act, everyone was shocked—but I wasn't. I was sure Erik had taken her, using one of his incredible tricks. I truly believed this could be the end—for Christine, for Erik, and for everyone else. I even thought about warning everyone to leave the building, but I knew they'd think I was crazy, so I stayed silent.

Instead, I decided to act immediately. I figured Erik's attention would be on Christine, giving me a chance to sneak into his home through the third cellar. I brought the young viscount with me. He was desperate, and he trusted me more than I expected. I had already sent my servant to fetch my pistols. I gave one to Raoul and told him to be ready—Erik might be waiting on the other side of the wall. We planned to go through the trapdoor and down the Communists' road.

When Raoul saw the pistols, he asked if we were going to fight a duel. I said, "Yes—and what a duel it will be." But there was no time to explain. He was brave, but he didn't know the danger we faced. That might've been for the best.

What scared me most was the thought that Erik could already be near, preparing his deadly weapon: the Punjab lasso. No one knows how to use it like he does. He is both a master magician and the king of stranglers. Back in the days of Mazenderan, when he entertained the little sultana, she would ask him to scare her with his tricks. That's when he introduced the terrible game of the Punjab lasso.

Erik had lived in India, where he became incredibly skilled at using a strangling rope called the Punjab lasso. People would lock him in a courtyard with a warrior—usually someone sentenced to death—who was given weapons like a long spear and a sword. Erik only had his lasso. Just when the warrior thought he had Erik cornered, the lasso would snap through the air. With a quick flick of his wrist, Erik would tighten the rope around the man's neck and drag him across the ground. He did this to impress the little sultana and her ladies, who watched from a nearby window and clapped for him. The sultana even learned to use the lasso herself and killed some of her own servants and friends with it.

But I'd rather not talk more about those dark days in Mazenderan. I only bring them up to explain why, when I brought the Vicomte de Chagny with me into the Opera's underground cellars, I was constantly on alert for Erik's deadly tricks. My pistols were useless against someone like Erik, especially since he'd never show himself. But the lasso? That could be used at any time.

I didn't have time to explain all of this to the viscount. Even if I had, it would've only made him more nervous. So I simply told him to keep one arm bent with his hand raised at eye level, just like someone preparing to fire a gun. When you keep that position, it's nearly impossible for even the best strangler to use the lasso effectively. The rope might catch your arm or hand, instead of your neck, giving you a chance to untangle it.

After sneaking past the police officer, the stagehands, firemen, the rat-catcher, and even the mysterious man in the felt hat without being seen, the viscount and I finally reached the third cellar. We stood between the old Roi de Lahore set piece and another piece of scenery. I worked the hidden stone in the wall, and we dropped down into Erik's secret house, which he had built himself within the thick foundation walls of the Opera. This was easy for him to do, since he had been one of the main builders under the architect, Philippe Garnier. He kept working in secret when the construction paused during the war and the Paris Commune.

I knew Erik too well to feel safe once we landed in his house. I remembered how he had turned an ordinary palace in Mazenderan into a terrifying place, full of listening walls, hidden passages, and deadly tricks. His worst invention was something called the torture chamber. Usually, no one entered it unless they were sentenced to death—or unless the sultana felt like torturing someone for fun. Victims could escape their suffering only by using the Punjab lasso or a bowstring, which Erik left hanging from an iron tree for that purpose.

That's why I felt a wave of fear when I realized the room we were in was an exact copy of that torture chamber. And there, at our feet, lay the very rope I had feared all night—the Punjab lasso. I was sure this was the same rope that killed Joseph Buquet. He had probably seen Erik using the hidden stone in the third cellar, tried it himself, and ended up trapped in this room, where he died.

I could easily imagine Erik dragging Joseph's body back to the Roi de Lahore set and hanging it there to scare others away from discovering his hiding place. Later, Erik must have returned to take the rope, since it could've raised suspicions if found during an investigation.

Now, seeing the rope lying at our feet in the torture room made me break into a cold sweat. As I moved the small red light from my lantern across the walls, I felt my heart race. The viscount noticed and asked, "What's wrong, sir?"

I quickly motioned for him to be quiet.

[1] An official report from Tonkin, received in Paris at the end of July, 1909, relates how the famous pirate chief De Tham was tracked, together with his men, by our soldiers; and how all of them succeeded in escaping, thanks to this trick of the reeds.

[2] DAROGA is Persian for chief of police.

[3] The Persian might easily have admitted that Erik's fate also interested himself, for he was well aware that, if the government of Teheran had learned that Erik was still alive, it would have been all up with the modest pension of the erstwhile daroga. It is only fair, however, to add that the Persian had a noble and generous heart; and I do not doubt for a moment that the catastrophes which he feared for others greatly occupied his mind. His conduct, throughout this business, proves it and is above all praise.

Chapter XXII
In the Torture Chamber

THE PERSIAN'S NARRATIVE CONTINUED

We stood in the center of a small, six-sided room. Every wall was completely covered in mirrors, from top to bottom. In the corners, we could see the edges where the mirrors met and the sections designed to rotate on hidden gears. I recognized them. I also saw the iron tree standing in one corner—an iron tree with a metal branch meant for hanging people.

I grabbed the viscount's arm. He was trembling all over, wanting to call out to Christine and tell her he was there to save her. I was afraid he wouldn't be able to hold himself back.

Then, suddenly, we heard a noise to our left. It sounded like a door opening and closing in the next room. A moment later, we heard a soft groan. I gripped the viscount's arm even tighter. And then we heard a voice say clearly:

"You must choose! A wedding mass or a funeral mass!"

It was Erik. I recognized his voice.

There was another low moan, followed by silence.

By now, I was sure Erik didn't know we were in his house. If he had known, he would never have let us hear him speak. He only had to close the tiny hidden window that looked down into this mirrored torture chamber. And if he had known we were here, I was certain he would have already started using his traps and torments.

The most important thing was to make sure he never realized we were here. I was especially worried that the viscount would do something impulsive—like try to break through the walls to get to Christine. We could still hear her soft cries every now and then.

Then Erik spoke again, his voice calmer:

"Funeral masses aren't much fun," he said. "But wedding masses— they're beautiful! You have to decide what you want. I can't live like this anymore, hiding away underground like a mole. Don Juan Triumphant is finished, and now I want to live a normal life. I want a wife like anyone else. I've even made a mask that makes me look normal. No one will stare at me on the street. You'll be so happy. We'll sing together until we faint from joy."

Then his voice changed, full of emotion.

"You're crying. You're scared of me. But I'm not evil. Just love me, and you'll see. I only ever wanted someone to love me for who I am. If you did, I'd be as gentle as a lamb. You could do anything you wanted with me."

The sounds of sobbing grew louder. But we were shocked to realize that it was Erik crying. It was heartbreaking. Christine seemed frozen in fear, unable to speak, while he knelt at her feet, begging.

Three times he cried out in agony:

"You don't love me! You don't love me! You don't love me!"

Then, more softly:

"Why are you crying? You know it hurts me to see you cry."

There was silence again.

Each time it grew quiet, we hoped that maybe he had left Christine alone. Maybe this was our chance to reach her. But we couldn't escape this mirrored chamber unless she opened the door from the other side. The problem was, we didn't even know where the door was.

Suddenly, we heard the ring of an electric bell in the next room. There was the sound of someone jumping up, and Erik's voice thundered:

"Someone's ringing! Come in, please!"

Then came a chilling laugh.

"Who's bothering me now? Wait here… I'm going to tell the siren to open the door."

We heard footsteps, and then a door closed. I didn't have time to wonder what terrible thing Erik might be planning next. All I could think about was one thing—Christine was now alone behind the wall.

The Vicomte de Chagny was already calling out:

"Christine! Christine!"

Since we could hear everything happening in the next room, it made sense that Christine would be able to hear him too. Still, Raoul had to call her name several times.

Finally, we heard a soft voice respond.

"I must be dreaming," it said.

"Christine, Christine, it's me—Raoul!" he called again.

There was a pause.

"Please answer me, Christine! For the love of heaven, if you're alone, say something!"

Then we heard Christine softly whisper Raoul's name.

"Yes, yes, it's really me!" he said. "You're not dreaming. Christine, trust me. We're here to save you. But be careful. If you hear Erik coming, let us know right away."

Christine sounded terrified. She was scared Erik would find out where Raoul was hiding. In a rush, she told us Erik had gone completely mad from love and had threatened to kill everyone—including himself—if she refused to marry him. He had given her until eleven o'clock the next night to make her choice. That was her last chance. As he told her, she had to choose between a wedding mass or a funeral mass.

Then Erik had said something that confused Christine:

"Yes or no! If you say no, everyone will be dead and buried!"

But I understood exactly what he meant—and it matched my worst fear.

"Can you tell where Erik is now?" I asked.

"He must have left the house," she answered.

"Can you be sure?" I asked again.

"No," she said. "I'm tied up. I can't move at all."

Hearing this, Raoul and I cried out in anger. Our only hope for escape—our only chance—depended on Christine being able to move freely.

"But where are you?" Christine asked. "There are only two doors in this room—the one Erik uses to come and go, and another that he's never opened in front of me. He told me never to touch it. He says it's the most dangerous door... the door to the torture chamber!"

"Christine—that's where we are!" I said.

"You're in the torture chamber?" she asked in disbelief.

"Yes, but we can't see the door from inside."

"Oh, if only I could reach it!" she cried. "I'd knock on the door so you'd know where it is."

"Does it have a lock?" I asked quickly.

"Yes, it has a lock."

"Mademoiselle," I said firmly, "you must find a way to open that door."

"But how?" she asked, her voice weak with frustration and tears.

We heard her struggling against the ropes that held her.

"I know where the key is," she said, breathless. "But he's tied me up so tightly... Oh, that awful man!"

She sobbed.

"Where is the key?" I asked. I motioned to Raoul to stay quiet and let me handle this—we didn't have time to waste.

"In the next room, near the organ," she said. "It's with another small bronze key. He keeps both of them in a little leather bag. He calls it the bag of life and death... Raoul! Raoul, get out while you still can! Everything here is strange and terrifying, and Erik is losing his mind! You're in the torture chamber! Go back the way you came. There has to be a reason it's called that!"

"Christine," Raoul replied. "We'll leave together, or we'll die together."

"We have to stay calm," I whispered. "Why did he tie you up, mademoiselle? He knows you can't escape from this place."

"I tried to take my own life," Christine said. "That monster left me here last night after bringing me in while I was faint and half-drugged. He said he was going to the bank. When he came back, he found me with blood on my face... I had tried to kill myself by slamming my head against the wall."

"Christine!" Raoul groaned, breaking into tears.

"Then he tied me up. He said I'm not allowed to die before eleven o'clock tomorrow night."

"Mademoiselle," I said firmly, "he tied you up—but he can untie you. You just have to play along for now. Don't forget that he loves you."

"Sadly," she said, "how could I forget?"

"Then use it. Smile at him, speak kindly, ask him to untie you. Tell him your restraints are hurting you."

But Christine whispered quickly, "Quiet... I hear something by the wall near the lake! It's him... go, go, go!"

"We couldn't leave even if we wanted to," I replied seriously. "We're trapped here... and we're in the torture room."

"Shh!" she said again.

Heavy footsteps echoed beyond the wall. The floor creaked under the weight. Then we heard a huge sigh—and a horrified gasp from Christine. Erik's voice followed:

"Sorry to let you see me like this! Don't I look awful? It's HIS fault! Why did he ring? Do I ask random people to tell me the time? He won't be asking anyone anything ever again! It's the siren's fault."

Another deep, soul-crushing sigh followed.

"Why did you scream, Christine?"

"Because I'm in pain, Erik."

"I thought I scared you."

"Erik, please untie me… Aren't I your prisoner?"

"You'll try to kill yourself again."

"You gave me until eleven o'clock tomorrow night, Erik."

His footsteps dragged slowly again.

"Since we're both going to die anyway… and I want it too… yes, I'm done with life… Don't move, I'll untie you. All you have to do is say one word: 'No!' And that's it—it ends for everyone. You're right, why wait until tomorrow night? Sure, it would've been more dramatic… but that's just childish. We should only think of ourselves. Nothing else matters… Are you staring at me because I'm soaked? Oh, Christine, it's pouring outside. Besides that, I think I'm seeing things. The man who rang the siren's bell just now—go check if he's still at the bottom of the lake—he looked like… Never mind. Turn around. Are you happy now? You're free… Oh, poor Christine, look at your wrists. Did I hurt you? That alone should cost me my life… Speaking of death, I must sing his requiem."

When I heard those horrible words, a terrible feeling crept over me… I remembered that I too had once rung that siren's bell. I must have triggered some kind of warning signal. And I remembered the two arms rising from the dark waters…

Who had wandered to that shore this time? Who was "the other one," the person whose requiem Erik was now singing?

Erik's voice thundered through the room as he sang the Dies Irae, shaking everything around us like a violent storm. It felt like the whole world was crashing in. Suddenly, the music and singing stopped so abruptly that Raoul jumped back in shock.

Then Erik's voice, colder and sharper, rang out in hard, metallic tones:

"WHAT HAVE YOU DONE WITH MY BAG?"

Chapter XXIII
The Tortures Begin

THE PERSIAN'S NARRATIVE CONTINUED

The angry voice shouted again, "What did you do with my bag? So that's why you asked me to untie you—so you could steal it!"

We heard quick footsteps—Christine was running back to the Louis-Philippe room, trying to get away and hide on the other side of the wall.

"Why are you running?" Erik yelled, chasing her. "Give me my bag! Don't you understand? That bag holds life and death!"

"Listen to me, Erik," Christine said softly. "Since it's decided we're going to live together... why does it matter anymore?"

"You know there are only two keys in that bag," Erik snapped. "What are you trying to do?"

"I just want to see the room you've always kept hidden from me," she said, trying to sound playful. "It's just woman's curiosity!"

But Erik wasn't fooled.

"I don't like curious women," he said coldly. "You'd better remember the story of Bluebeard and be careful... Now give me my bag! Give it to me! Stay away from that key, you nosy little thing!"

He laughed darkly, and Christine cried out in pain. Erik had clearly grabbed the bag back from her.

At that moment, Raoul couldn't hold back his anger and made a sound of frustration.

"What was that?" said Erik sharply. "Did you hear that, Christine?"

"No, no," she said quickly. "I didn't hear anything."

"I thought I heard someone cry out."

"A cry? Are you going mad, Erik? Who could cry out in this house? I only screamed because you hurt me! I heard nothing else."

"I don't like the way you said that," Erik growled. "You're shaking... You're nervous... You're lying! That was a cry! Someone's in the torture chamber! Oh, now I get it!"

"There's no one there, Erik!"

"Oh, yes! I understand now!"

"There's no one!"

"It must be the man you want to marry!"

"I don't want to marry anyone! You know I don't."

Erik let out another awful laugh. "Well, we'll see about that very soon. Christine, my darling, we don't need to open the door to find out what's going on in the torture chamber. Would you like to see for yourself? Do you want to know if anyone's in there? It's easy—you'll see the invisible window light up near the ceiling. All we have to do is pull the black curtain and turn off the light in here. There we go... Let's turn out the light. You're not afraid of the dark, are you? Not when you're with your little husband!"

Then we heard Christine cry out in fear:

"No! I'm scared! I told you—I hate the dark! I don't care about that room anymore. You're always scaring me with stories about your torture chamber. I got curious, but now I don't care. Not one bit!"

And just like I feared, everything changed in an instant. The whole room we were in suddenly lit up, as if someone had turned on a powerful light. Everything around us was glowing. The Vicomte de Chagny was so shocked, he nearly stumbled backward. Then we heard Erik's angry voice shout:

"I told you someone was there! Look up—see that small window lit near the ceiling? The person inside can't see it, but you can! Now you understand what those folding steps are for. You've asked me about them so many times. Well, they're so you can peek into the torture chamber... you little busybody!"

"Torture? Who's being tortured? Erik—please—tell me this is just one of your tricks! Say you're only trying to scare me! If you love me, say there's no one being tortured!"

"Go on, take a look through the little window, my dear."

I don't know if Raoul heard her soft voice—he was completely focused on the disturbing scene in front of him. As for me, I had seen it all before, back in Mazenderan. I wasn't watching—I was listening, waiting for a clue about what to do next.

"Look through the window! Tell me what he looks like!"

We heard something being moved across the floor—Christine was being led to the steps.

"Go up! No? Then I'll go myself."

"Oh, fine. I'll do it. Let me."

"Oh, how sweet of you! Saving me the trouble at my age. Now, tell me—what does he look like?"

Then, just above us, we heard Christine's voice clearly:

"There's no one there!"

"No one? Are you sure?"

"Yes, I'm sure. No one's there."

"Well, that's good! What's wrong, Christine? You're not going to faint now, are you—since there's no one there? Come on, climb down... there you go. Take a breath. Feel better? That's it! You're fine now! Now, tell me—what do you think of the scenery?"

"Oh... it's beautiful."

"That's better. You're feeling calmer now, aren't you? No need to panic. Isn't this a funny little house, with rooms like that?"

"Yes, it's like a wax museum... But Erik, are you really sure there's no torture going on in there? You scared me so much!"

"Then why would there be torture, if there's no one inside?"

"Did you design that room yourself? It's impressive. You're really talented, Erik."

"Yes, I am—at least in my own way."

"But then... why do you call it the torture chamber?"

"Oh, that's simple. What did you see in there?"

"A forest."

"And what do forests have?"

"Trees."

"And what do you usually find in trees?"

"Birds."

"Did you see any birds?"

"No... there weren't any birds."

"Then what did you see? Think! You saw branches. And what do branches become?" His voice turned cold. "A gallows. That's why I call it my torture chamber! It's just a joke. I don't talk like most people. But honestly... I'm tired of it all! I'm sick of this house with all its fake rooms and secret walls. I want a normal home. Just a regular apartment, with real doors and windows... and a wife inside who loves me. Someone I can take on walks on Sundays... someone I can make laugh during the week. Want me to show you a card trick? That'll help pass the time until eleven tomorrow night. My sweet Christine... are you listening? Tell me you love me! No? That's okay... you will. At first, you couldn't even look at my mask because you knew what was behind it. Now, you can stare right at it and forget what's underneath. See? People can get used to anything—if they try. Lots of people didn't love each other before marriage, but they grew to love each other later. I don't even know what I'm saying anymore. But you'd have fun with me. I'm the best ventriloquist in the world! You're laughing... You don't believe me? Listen..."

The awful man, who really was the best ventriloquist in the world, was only trying to distract Christine from what was happening in the torture room. But it was a foolish plan, because all Christine could think about was us. In the sweetest voice she could manage, she kept begging him:

"Please, turn off the light in the little window! Erik, please turn it off!"

She knew that the sudden light he spoke about so threateningly had to mean something terrible. Still, she must've felt a little better seeing that Raoul and I were alive, standing in that bright light behind the wall. But she would've felt much safer if the light had gone out completely.

While this was happening, Erik began one of his ventriloquist tricks.

"Here," he said, "I'm lifting my mask just a little… oh, just a bit! Can you see my lips? Well, they're not moving! My mouth isn't open, and still, you hear my voice. Want it in your left ear? Your right? In the table? In one of those little black boxes on the mantel?"

"Listen—now it's coming from the box on the right. What do you hear it say? 'SHOULD I TURN THE SCORPION?' And now—snap! It's in the box on the left. What does that one say? 'SHOULD I TURN THE GRASSHOPPER?' Snap! Now it's inside the little leather bag. What's it saying now? 'I AM THE LITTLE BAG OF LIFE AND DEATH!'"

"Now—snap! It's in Carlotta's throat. Yes, her beautiful voice! What's it saying? 'It's me, Mr. Toad! I sing without fear—co-ack!—let the music take me—co-ack!' And now—snap! It's on the chair in the ghost's box! And it says, 'MADAME CARLOTTA IS SINGING TONIGHT TO MAKE THE CHANDELIER FALL!' And now— snap! Can you guess where Erik's voice is now? Listen, Christine, sweetheart! It's behind the door to the torture room! It's me, inside the torture room! And what am I saying? I'm saying, 'Watch out, anyone with a real nose, if you dare peek inside the torture chamber! Aha, aha, aha!'"

Erik's terrifying voice came from everywhere at once. It seemed to echo from the invisible window, bounce through the walls, circle around us, even pass between us. He was right there, speaking directly to us! We tried to move, ready to fight him—but his voice vanished as quickly as it came, slipping behind the wall like a ghostly echo.

Then it all went silent. And this is what happened next:

"Erik! Erik!" cried Christine. "Your voice is wearing me out. Please stop. Erik, isn't it getting really hot in here?"

"Oh yes," Erik replied. "It's boiling in here."

"But… why? The wall is hot—it's actually burning!"

"I'll tell you, Christine, darling—it's because of the forest next door."

"What does that have to do with anything? A forest?"

"DIDN'T YOU SEE? IT'S AN AFRICAN FOREST!"

Then he let out a loud, horrible laugh—so awful that we couldn't hear Christine's cries anymore. Raoul lost control and started yelling and beating his fists against the walls like he'd gone crazy. I tried to stop him, but it was useless. Erik's horrible laugh drowned everything out, even for himself.

Then we heard a heavy thud, like a body hitting the floor... being dragged... a door slammed shut... and then—nothing.

Only heat. And a silence so thick and hot, it felt like we were trapped in the middle of a burning jungle.

Chapter XXIV
"Barrels! ... Barrels! ... Any Barrels to Sell?"

THE PERSIAN'S NARRATIVE CONTINUED

The room where the Vicomte de Chagny and I were trapped was a perfect six-sided space, and every wall was covered with mirrors. These kinds of rooms have become more common now, especially at fairs and exhibitions, where they're called things like "illusion palaces." But Erik was the one who invented the very first one. I saw him build it with my own eyes during the time we spent in Mazenderan.

At first, it was just for fun. He'd place something simple, like a column, in one corner, and the mirrors would reflect it over and over, making it look like you were standing in a grand hall filled with hundreds of columns. Each mirror made the room appear to stretch into six other rooms, and each of those looked like it stretched even farther. But the little sultana got bored with that trick, so Erik changed it into something far more disturbing—a torture room.

Instead of a column, he put an iron tree in the corner. It was painted to look real, with leaves and branches, but it was made of solid metal, so no one could break it or tear it down, no matter how hard they tried. We'll soon see how this same room could be instantly transformed into two different settings, just by rotating special drums hidden in the corners. Each drum had three sections with different scenery painted on them. As the drums turned, the new images came into view, changing the whole room in seconds.

The walls offered no help to anyone trapped inside. There was nothing to grip or break, because everything was smooth mirror, except for the one solid object in the corner. And victims were thrown into this room with nothing on their feet and nothing in their hands.

There was no furniture, but the ceiling could be lit up. Erik had also built a clever heating system. It could make the walls and air inside the room as hot as a burning jungle, something modern systems later copied.

I'm explaining all of this—how a few painted leaves and clever mirrors could create the illusion of a burning rainforest—so that no one will think I'm insane or making things up. What Erik built was real. It was terrible, but it was real.

Now, let's go back to where I left off. When the ceiling lights came on and the forest seemed to grow all around us, Raoul was completely shocked. He stared at the trees, frozen in disbelief. He rubbed his forehead like he was trying to wake up from a nightmare. His eyes fluttered, and for a moment, he couldn't even listen to what was happening next door.

I wasn't surprised by the scene—I'd seen it before. So I focused on listening to what was going on in the next room. But something else caught my eye: the mirrors. Some were cracked and scratched. Even though they were made strong enough to withstand attacks, someone had damaged them. This told me the chamber had already been used to torture someone before.

That poor soul, whoever he was, must not have been barefoot like the victims in Mazenderan. He had probably stumbled into this terrifying illusion, panicked, and kicked out at the mirrors in fury. And the tree where he ended his suffering was placed so he could see himself dying... while the mirrors reflected not just his pain, but what looked like a thousand others suffering right along with him.

Yes, Joseph Buquet had definitely gone through this same nightmare. Were we going to die like he did? I didn't think so. I knew we still had a few hours left, and I planned to use them better than Joseph had. I was familiar with most of Erik's tricks, and if there was ever a time to use that knowledge, it was now.

First, I gave up all hope of escaping through the passage we'd come from. Trying to reach the stone from inside the chamber was impossible. We had dropped from too high up into this terrible room. There was no furniture to climb on, not even the iron tree or each other's shoulders could help us reach that high.

The only possible way out was the hidden door that led to the room where Erik and Christine were. But while it looked like a regular door on their side, we couldn't see it at all from where we were. That meant we had to try and open a door without knowing exactly where it was.

Once I was certain there was no hope of help from Christine—especially after I heard Erik dragging her away to keep her from interfering—I decided it was time to act.

But first, I had to calm the Vicomte de Chagny, who was panicking and shouting nonsense. The parts of Erik and Christine's conversation he had overheard only made things worse. On top of that, the strange, burning forest illusion and the rising heat made him sweat and shake uncontrollably. He shouted Christine's name, waved his pistol around, and even rammed his head against the mirrors, trying to "run" through the fake forest. The torture was already starting to affect his mind.

I tried my best to make him listen to reason. I made him touch the mirrors, the iron tree, and the branches. I explained how the illusion worked—that it was just a trick with lights and mirrors, and that we didn't have to fall for it like others might.

"We're just in a room," I told him. "A small room. That's what you have to keep telling yourself. And we'll get out of it—as soon as we find the door."

I promised him that if he let me work quietly without interrupting me by yelling or pacing, I would find the door's trick within an hour.

He finally lay down on the floor like someone resting in a forest and said he would wait there until I found the door. Then he added, "The view from here is beautiful!" The illusion was getting to him, even if he didn't fully realize it.

Ignoring the forest, I went straight to one of the glass panels and started feeling it carefully. I was looking for the exact spot that would activate the door—a hidden spring, probably no bigger than a pea. Erik used a pivot system for his doors, and I figured he would've placed the trigger at a height that matched his own.

I slowly searched the panels, moving as quickly as I could despite the unbearable heat. We were practically baking inside this glowing forest. After working for half an hour and finishing three panels, I suddenly turned around when the viscount groaned:

"I can't breathe," he said. "The heat from all these mirrors is awful! Do you think you'll find that spring soon? If you take too long, we'll be cooked alive in here!"

I was actually relieved to hear him talk like that. At least he wasn't mentioning the forest anymore. I hoped he was still holding onto his sanity.

But then he added, "What makes me feel a little better is knowing that Erik gave Christine until eleven tomorrow night. If we can't escape and help her, at least we'll be dead before she is! Then Erik's funeral music can be for all three of us!"

He gasped for air—so hot it nearly knocked him out.

Unlike the viscount, I wasn't ready to give up and accept death. After giving him a few words of encouragement, I went back to work. But I'd made a mistake. I had moved while talking to him, and now, in the confusing maze of the fake forest, I couldn't find the panel I had been working on. I had to start all over, blindly searching again.

Soon the heat started to get to me too. I searched and searched, but found nothing. The other room was silent. We were lost—no exit, no sense of direction, no plan. I knew what would happen if no one came to save us... or if I didn't find the secret switch. But no matter how hard I looked, all I found were fake branches—realistic, sure, but offering no shade or help. That made sense; we were in an illusion of an African jungle, with a burning sun straight overhead.

The viscount and I kept taking off our coats and putting them back on, trying to figure out if we felt cooler without them or more protected with them. I was still fighting to stay calm, but he looked completely gone. He began mumbling that he'd been walking through this forest for three days and nights, searching for Christine. Sometimes, he imagined he saw her slipping between the trees, and he called to her, begging her to come to him. His voice made my eyes fill with tears.

Then, suddenly, he cried out, "I'm so thirsty!"

I was too. My throat felt like it was on fire. But even as I crouched on the floor, I kept searching for the switch to the hidden door... I knew we needed to escape before nightfall. Night in an equatorial forest is dangerous—especially if you can't build a fire to keep away wild animals. I had even tried to snap off a branch to use as kindling, but I hit the mirror instead and remembered—none of this was real.

When night fell, the heat didn't go away. In fact, it got worse, glowing hotter under the strange, bluish moonlight. I told the viscount to keep his gun ready and stay close while I kept searching for the switch.

Then we heard it—a lion's roar, not far off.

"He's close," the viscount whispered. "Don't you see him? Over there… in the bushes! If he roars again, I'm shooting!"

The roar came again, even louder. The viscount fired his gun. I don't think he hit anything—but he did shatter one of the mirrors. I saw the damage the next morning. We must have stumbled a long way during the night, because suddenly we found ourselves in a different illusion—an endless desert of sand and rocks. Leaving the jungle just to end up in a desert felt like a cruel joke.

Exhausted, I collapsed next to the viscount. I was done hunting for switches that didn't exist.

I said to him that I was surprised we hadn't come across more animals. Usually, after a lion, there would be a leopard or even the annoying buzz of a tsetse fly. All of it was staged, of course. I explained how Erik made those sounds—using a large drum made with donkey hide, a string of catgut, and a resin-covered glove. Depending on how he rubbed the string, he could perfectly mimic a lion, a leopard, or even a buzzing fly.

Knowing Erik was probably sitting right next door, creating all this, made me want to try talking to him. There was no point in pretending we could catch him off guard anymore—he definitely knew we were in his torture room. So I called out: "Erik! Erik!"

I yelled as loud as I could into the empty desert... but nothing answered. Just silence, stretching endlessly around us.

What were we going to do in this horrible, lonely place?

We were slowly dying—of heat, hunger, and worst of all, thirst. Finally, I saw the viscount lift himself up a bit and point off into the distance. He had spotted something on the horizon.

An oasis.

Yes, far off in the distance, we saw what looked like an oasis—clear water reflecting the iron trees. But I knew better. It was just another illusion. I recognized it right away. This was the worst trick of all, the one no one could resist. Everyone who'd seen it had fallen for it. I fought hard to stay calm and not let myself believe it was real water. I knew what would happen if someone hoped for water, reached it, and then realized it wasn't real—there would only be one thing left to do: hang themselves on the iron tree.

So I shouted to Raoul:

"It's a mirage! Don't believe it! It's fake, just another trick with mirrors!"

But he snapped at me. He told me to stop with my nonsense about mirrors and hidden switches and tricks. He was angry, saying I must be blind or insane if I couldn't see the water—so real, flowing between the trees. And he insisted the desert was real, the forest was real, and he wasn't a fool. He said he'd traveled the world and knew what he was seeing.

Then he dragged himself forward, calling, "Water! Water!" His mouth hung open like he could already taste it.

Mine did too.

Because it wasn't just what we saw. We heard the water. We heard it flowing, bubbling, trickling. You don't just hear that kind of sound with your ears—it gets into your mouth, your throat. You stick out your tongue just to try and feel it better.

And worst of all—we heard rain. But there was no rain.

That sound was one of Erik's cruelest inventions. He used a long, narrow box filled with tiny stones and rough wooden and metal pieces inside. When the stones dropped, they bounced around and made a pattering noise, just like a rainstorm.

We dragged ourselves toward the "riverbank," our eyes and ears filled with the sound and sight of water... but our mouths were dry and cracked.

When we reached the mirror, Raoul licked it. So did I.

It burned our tongues. The glass was hot.

Then we collapsed on the floor and cried out in despair. Raoul put the pistol—our last loaded one—against his head. I stared at the Punjab lasso hanging from the iron tree. Now I understood why the iron tree had returned in this final illusion—it was waiting for me.

But just then, something caught my eye and made me jump. Raoul paused before pulling the trigger. I grabbed his arm, took the pistol away, and crawled toward what I had seen.

Near the lasso, hidden in a groove in the floor, was a black-headed nail. I knew what it was. It was the hidden switch. I touched it. I turned to Raoul with a face full of hope. I pressed it.

And instead of a door opening in the wall, a trapdoor opened in the floor.

A wave of cool air rose up from the darkness below. We leaned over it, breathing it in like fresh water. We couldn't see what was down there, but it felt like standing at the edge of a deep well.

I reached my arm into the opening and felt stone steps leading down.

Raoul wanted to throw himself into the hole right away, but I stopped him. I turned on my lantern and went first, afraid Erik had set another trap.

The stone stairs twisted downward, and the cool air was a relief after the suffocating heat. We figured the lake had to be nearby.

At the bottom, our eyes began to adjust, and we saw shapes around us—round ones. I shined the lantern and realized they were barrels.

We were in Erik's cellar. This must be where he kept his wine... and hopefully water.

Raoul started patting the barrels and saying, "Barrels! So many barrels!"

They were all small and neatly lined up in two rows. Erik must've chosen small ones so he could easily move them to his home on the lake.

We checked each one for signs it had been opened. None had. I lifted one to make sure it was full, then got out a small knife to open the plug.

Just as I started to dig at the barrel's opening, I heard something—a faint chant coming from far away. It was a familiar sound I'd heard on the streets of Paris:

"Barrels! Barrels! Any barrels to sell?"

I froze. Raoul heard it too.

"That's strange," he said. "It sounds like... like the barrel is singing."

The voice sang again, fainter:

"Barrels! Barrels! Any barrels to sell?"

"It's like the sound is coming from the barrel," Raoul whispered.

We looked behind it—nothing. Still, we felt like the sound had come from inside. We were starting to wonder if we were losing our minds.

I returned to the plug. Raoul cupped his hands under it, and with one last push, I burst it open.

"What's this?" he cried. "This isn't water!"

He held the contents near the lantern. I bent down to look.

Then I threw the lantern to the ground so hard it shattered—and the light went out.

What I saw in Raoul's hands... was gunpowder.

[1] It is very natural that, at the time when the Persian was writing, he should take so many precautions against any spirit of incredulity on the part of those who were likely to read his narrative. Nowadays, when we have all seen this sort of room, his precautions would be superfluous.

Chapter XXV
The Scorpion or the Grasshopper: Which?

THE PERSIAN'S NARRATIVE CONCLUDED

The discovery filled us with a fear so intense that we forgot all the pain and suffering we'd already gone through. Now we understood what the Phantom meant when he told Christine:

"Yes or no! If your answer is no, everyone will be dead and buried!"

He wasn't speaking in riddles. He meant it—buried beneath the ruins of the Paris Opera House.

He had given Christine until eleven o'clock tomorrow night. He chose the timing carefully. The theater would be full—crowded with people. What better funeral could he ask for than one surrounded by sparkling jewels and elegant gowns?

Eleven o'clock tomorrow night.

We would all be blown to pieces during the performance—if Christine said no.

Eleven o'clock tomorrow night.

But what else could she say but no? How could she agree to marry a man who looked like a living corpse? She didn't realize that her answer would decide the fate of hundreds of people.

Eleven o'clock tomorrow night.

We crawled through the dark, trying to find the stone staircase. The light that had once shone through the trapdoor above us had gone out. As we felt our way forward, we kept repeating:

"Eleven o'clock tomorrow night."

Finally, I found the staircase. But I froze on the first step. A horrible thought struck me:

"What time is it now?"

Yes—what if it was already eleven? What if the time was now?

How could we know? It felt like we had been trapped there for days—maybe even years. Maybe the explosion was about to happen right then.

Suddenly, we heard something—a sharp sound, like something cracking.

"Did you hear that?" I cried. "There—in the corner! That sounded like machinery! Another crack! Could it be the mechanism that's going to blow us up?"

We both panicked. Fear drove us to rush up the steps, tripping as we went. We just wanted to get away, to escape that terrible darkness and reach the mirrored room above.

We found the trapdoor still open, but it was just as dark in the mirror room as in the cellar. We crawled across the floor, directly above the barrels of gunpowder.

What time was it?

We shouted—Raoul called for Christine, and I yelled for Erik. I reminded him that I had once saved his life. But there was no answer—only the echo of our fear and madness.

We tried to figure out how long we had been there, but we couldn't think clearly anymore. If only we could see a clock—just once.

My watch had stopped, but Raoul's was still ticking. He had wound it before dressing for the opera. We had no matches or light of any kind, but we had to try. Raoul broke the glass of his watch and felt the hands with his fingers. Based on where they were, he guessed it might be just eleven o'clock.

But which eleven o'clock? Was it the right one? Or did we still have twelve hours left?

Then I suddenly said, "Quiet!"

I thought I heard footsteps in the next room. A gentle tap on the wall. And then Christine's voice:

"Raoul! Raoul!"

We all started talking at once, shouting through the wall. Christine was crying. She had feared Raoul was already dead.

She told us that Erik had been acting terribly—shouting, threatening everyone unless she agreed to marry him. She had promised to say yes if he would just let her into the torture chamber. But he refused and kept threatening to destroy everyone.

Finally, after what felt like endless hours, he had left her alone— giving her one last chance to think about her answer.

We were frozen in fear. Christine had said Erik gave her until eleven o'clock. But what time was it now?

"What time is it, Christine?" I asked.

"It's eleven! Just five minutes before!"

"But which eleven o'clock?" I said.

"The one that decides life or death," she answered. "That's what he said. Just before he left, he went mad. He tore off his mask—his yellow eyes were like fire! He laughed and said, 'I'm giving you five minutes to save yourself from shame. Here,' and he took a little bronze key from that terrible bag he calls the bag of life and death, 'this key opens the two black boxes on the mantel in the Louis-Philippe room. Inside, one has a scorpion and the other a grasshopper, both made of bronze. Whichever one you turn will give me your answer. Turn the scorpion, and it means yes. The grasshopper means no.' Then he laughed again, like a madman. I begged him to let me into the torture chamber, told him I'd marry him if he gave me the key. But he said he didn't need that key anymore and planned to throw it into the lake. And again he laughed and left. His last words were, 'The grasshopper! Watch out for the grasshopper! It doesn't just turn—it jumps! And it jumps very high!'"

Time was almost up, and those two symbols—scorpion and grasshopper—felt like they were clawing at my mind. I realized that if the grasshopper was turned, it would "hop"—and trigger an explosion. It was connected to a bomb.

Raoul had recovered his senses after hearing Christine's voice. He quickly explained to her what was happening—that turning the wrong figure could destroy everyone in the Opera House. He told her to turn the scorpion immediately.

There was a pause.

"Christine!" I shouted. "Where are you?"

"By the scorpion," she answered.

"Don't touch it!" I said quickly.

A horrible thought had struck me. What if Erik had tricked her again? What if the scorpion was the one that would cause the explosion? Why hadn't he returned by now? The five minutes were already up. Maybe he had hidden somewhere, waiting for the blast.

"Don't touch the scorpion!" I said again.

"I hear him! He's coming!" Christine cried.

We heard Erik's footsteps as he entered the room. He didn't speak at first. So I called out:

"Erik! It's me. Do you recognize my voice?"

He replied calmly, "So you're still alive in there? Then stay quiet."

I tried to speak again, but he interrupted coldly:

"Not a word, daroga, or I'll blow everything up."

Then he turned back to Christine.

"It's all in your hands, mademoiselle," he said slowly. "You haven't touched the scorpion... and you haven't touched the grasshopper. But it's not too late to make the right choice."

He opened the caskets with ease. "Look," he said. "Aren't they lovely? The scorpion and the grasshopper. If you turn the grasshopper, we all go up in flames. There's enough gunpowder under us to wipe out a whole quarter of Paris. But if you turn the scorpion, the water will come and flood the powder. Christine, with your own hands, you'll save hundreds of people sitting upstairs right now, watching that opera. And then—we'll get married."

He paused.

"If, in two minutes, you haven't turned the scorpion, I will turn the grasshopper. And remember—grasshoppers jump very high!"

Silence filled the air. Raoul dropped to his knees and began to pray. My heart pounded so hard I thought it might burst. Then Erik spoke again:

"Time's up... Goodbye, mademoiselle. Hop, grasshopper!"

"Erik!" Christine cried. "Do you swear—the scorpion is the right one?"

"Yes, it jumps at our wedding," he answered.

"You said it jumps!"

"At our wedding, dear child! The scorpion opens the ball. But that's enough! You won't choose the scorpion? Then I'll turn the grasshopper!"

"Erik!" we both shouted.

"I turned the scorpion!" Christine cried out.

That moment felt like it lasted forever. We waited, bracing ourselves for the explosion. We heard something move beneath us... a terrible hissing noise, like the start of a rocket.

It got louder. But it wasn't fire—it was water! Gurgling water!

We rushed to the trapdoor. Our thirst, which had been forgotten in our fear, returned instantly. The water rose fast from the cellar. It climbed over the barrels—the ones filled with gunpowder.

"Barrels! Barrels! Any barrels to sell?" That old chant echoed in our minds.

We went down to the water. It rose to our chins, our mouths, and we drank. We drank like we had never drunk before.

Then, in the dark, step by step, we followed the water as it rose. We climbed back up the stairs.

The water came out of the cellar with us and spread over the floor of the room. If, this went on, the whole house on the lake would be swamped. The floor of the torture-chamber had itself become a regular little lake, in which our feet splashed. Surely there was water enough now! Erik must turn off the tap!

"Erik! Erik! That is water enough for the gunpowder! Turn off the tap! Turn off the scorpion!"

But Erik did not reply. We heard nothing but the water rising: it was half-way to our waists!

"Christine!" cried M. de Chagny. "Christine! The water is up to our knees!"

But Christine did not reply ... We heard nothing but the water rising.

No one, no one in the next room, no one to turn the tap, no one to turn the scorpion!

We were all alone, in the dark, with the dark water that seized us and clasped us and froze us!

"Erik! Erik!"

"Christine! Christine!"

By this time, we had lost our foothold and were spinning round in the water, carried away by an irresistible whirl, for the water turned with us and dashed us against the dark mirror, which thrust us back again; and our throats, raised above the whirlpool, roared aloud.

Were we to die here, drowned in the torture-chamber? I had never seen that. Erik, at the time of the rosy hours of Mazenderan, had never shown me that, through the little invisible window.

"Erik! Erik!" I cried. "I saved your life! Remember! ... You were sentenced to death! But for me, you would be dead now! ... Erik!"

We whirled around in the water like so much wreckage. But, suddenly, my straying hands seized the trunk of the iron tree! I called M. de Chagny, and we both hung to the branch of the iron tree.

And the water rose still higher.

"Oh! Oh! Can you remember? How much space is there between the branch of the tree and the dome-shaped ceiling? Do try to remember! ... After all, the water may stop, it must find its level! ... There, I think it is stopping! ... No, no, oh, horrible! ... Swim! Swim for your life!"

Our arms became entangled in the effort of swimming; we choked; we fought in the dark water; already we could hardly breathe the dark air above the dark water, the air which escaped, which we could hear escaping through some vent-hole or other.

"Oh, let us turn and turn and turn until we find the air hole and then glue our mouths to it!"

But I lost my strength; I tried to lay hold of the walls! Oh, how those glass walls slipped from under my groping fingers! ... We whirled round again! ... We began to sink! ... One last effort! ... A last cry: "Erik! ... Christine! ..."

"Guggle, guggle, guggle!" in our ears. "Guggle! Guggle!" At the bottom of the dark water, our ears went, "Guggle! Guggle!"

And, before losing consciousness entirely, I seemed to hear, between two guggles:

"Barrels! Barrels! Any barrels to sell?"

Chapter XXVI

The End of the Ghost's Love Story

THE PERSIAN'S NARRATIVE CONCLUDED

The last part of the Persian's written account ends here.

Even though it seemed like there was no hope and that they were going to die, Raoul and the Persian were saved—thanks to Christine Daaé's incredible bravery and love. I learned the rest of the story directly from the Persian himself.

When I visited him, he was still living in a small apartment on Rue de Rivoli, across from the Tuileries Garden. He was very ill, and it took a lot of effort on my part to convince him to talk about the terrible events he had gone through. His loyal servant, Darius, brought me in. The Persian was sitting by a window that looked out at the garden. His eyes were still as striking as ever, but his face looked tired and worn. His head was shaved, which was usually hidden under his fur hat. He wore a long, plain coat and nervously twisted his thumbs in his sleeves. Still, his mind was sharp, and he told me the rest of the story clearly and calmly.

He said that when he woke up, he found himself lying in a bed. Raoul was nearby, resting on a sofa. Watching over them were two figures—one like an angel and the other like a devil.

After everything they had experienced in the torture room, the ordinary details of this small, cozy space seemed so strange it was almost unreal. It looked like a normal room in a modest home: a simple wooden bed, shiny mahogany chairs, a chest of drawers with brass handles, little cloth covers on the backs of the chairs, a clock on the mantel, and two small black boxes at each end. There was even a little shelf full of decorative items—seashells, red pin cushions, a mother-of-pearl boat, and a giant ostrich egg—lit softly by a shaded lamp on a round table. The peaceful, everyday look of the room, deep down in the cellars of the Opera, was even more confusing than all the frightening things that had come before.

And standing in that neat, homey room, the masked man—Erik—looked even more out of place, more intimidating. He leaned over the Persian and whispered:

"Are you feeling better, daroga? You're looking at my furniture, aren't you? It's all I have left from my poor mother."

Christine didn't say anything. She moved quietly, like a nurse who had taken a vow to never speak. She brought over a cup of something warm—maybe tea, maybe some kind of tonic. Erik took it from her and handed it to the Persian. Raoul was still asleep.

Erik added a bit of rum to the cup and, pointing to Raoul, said:

"He woke up before we even knew if you were going to make it, daroga. He's doing fine. He's just sleeping now. Let's not wake him."

Then Erik left the room for a short time. The Persian, weak but awake, looked around and saw Christine sitting quietly by the fireplace. He tried to speak to her, to call her name, but he didn't have the strength. Christine came over, touched his forehead gently, and then returned to her seat. The Persian noticed that she didn't even glance at Raoul—though he was sleeping peacefully—and she sat back down in silence, like a nurse who has taken a vow not to speak.

Erik came back carrying several small bottles, which he placed on the mantel. He sat down again, took the Persian's pulse, and whispered:

"You're both safe now. And soon, I'll take you back up to the surface. I'm doing it for my wife."

And with that, he stood up without saying anything more and left the room again.

The Persian looked at Christine's calm face in the soft light. She was quietly reading a small book with gold-edged pages, the kind that looked like a prayer book. The Persian couldn't stop thinking about the way Erik had softly said, "to please my wife." He gently tried calling Christine again, but she was so focused on her book that she didn't hear him.

Erik came back and gave the Persian some medicine. He told him not to speak to "his wife" or to anyone else, because it might be dangerous for everyone.

Eventually, the Persian fell asleep, just like Raoul had, and didn't wake up until he was back in his own room. His loyal servant Darius was taking care of him and explained that, the night before, someone had left the Persian at his front door. The stranger had rung the bell and then disappeared.

When the Persian felt better, he sent someone to Count Philippe's home to ask about Raoul. The reply was shocking: Raoul had not been seen, and Count Philippe was dead. His body had been found by the lake underneath the Opera House, on the Rue Scribe side.

The Persian remembered hearing the funeral music through the torture chamber wall and realized who was behind the crime. He knew Erik well enough to piece together what must have happened. Philippe probably thought his brother had run away with Christine Daaé, so he chased after them, heading toward Brussels, where he believed the elopement was planned. When he didn't find them there, he rushed back to the Opera. He remembered Raoul's strange comments about his mysterious rival and soon learned that Raoul had tried to get into the cellars and then vanished—leaving behind only his hat and an empty pistol case in Christine's dressing room. Philippe, now convinced that his brother had lost his mind, went underground himself.

This explained, in the Persian's mind, why Philippe's body had been found near the lake where Erik's siren kept watch.

The Persian didn't hesitate—he went straight to the police. The case was handled by a judge named Faure, a man who, in the Persian's opinion, was shallow, narrow-minded, and unwilling to believe anything out of the ordinary. He listened to the Persian's statement but treated him like a madman.

Frustrated and desperate, the Persian decided to write everything down. If the police wouldn't believe him, maybe the press would. He had just finished writing the account when Darius came in to say that a stranger was at the door. The man refused to give his name or show his face but insisted on speaking with the Persian and wouldn't leave.

The Persian immediately knew who it was and told Darius to let him in. He was right—it was Erik.

Erik looked very weak and leaned on the wall for support. He took off his hat to reveal a pale forehead, but the rest of his face was hidden behind his mask.

The Persian stood up when Erik entered and shouted, "Murderer of Count Philippe! What have you done with his brother and Christine Daaé?"

Erik seemed shaken by the accusation. He didn't answer right away, then slowly made his way to a chair and let out a deep sigh. He spoke in short, breathless phrases:

"Daroga... don't speak... of Count Philippe... He was already dead... when I left the house... He died... when the siren sang... It was... an accident... a sad, very sad... accident. He fell... into the lake... awkwardly... but naturally."

"You're lying!" the Persian snapped.

Erik lowered his head and said, "I didn't come here... to talk about Count Philippe... I came... to tell you... that I'm going to die."

"Where are Raoul de Chagny and Christine Daaé?"

"I'm going to die."

"Where are they?" the Persian demanded.

"Of love... daroga... I'm dying of love. That's what's happening. I loved her so much... I still do... And I'm dying because of it... If you only knew how beautiful she looked... when she let me kiss her... alive... It was the first time... the first time I'd ever kissed a woman... Yes... alive... I kissed her while she was alive... and she looked just as beautiful as if she had been dead."

The Persian grabbed Erik by the arm. "Tell me—Is she alive or dead?"

"Why are you shaking me?" Erik asked, trying to speak more clearly. "I told you... I'm going to die. Yes, I kissed her alive..."

"And now—is she dead?"

"I kissed her... on the forehead... and she didn't pull away... not even once."

Oh, she's a good girl! As for whether she's dead—no, I don't think so. But that's not up to me. No, she's alive! And I won't let anyone harm her, not even a little. She's kind and honest, and she saved your life, daroga, when I was ready to let you die. Honestly, no one else cared about you. Why were you even there with that young man? You would've died just like him! I swear, she begged me so hard for his life. But I told her that, since she turned the scorpion, she had agreed—on her own—to marry me. So there was no need for her to be promised to two men at once. That would've been ridiculous.

As for you, daroga, in my mind, you didn't exist anymore. You were already as good as dead, along with the other one. But when you were screaming like crazy because of the rising water, Christine came to me. Her big blue eyes were wide open, and she swore—on her life—that she agreed to be my wife. A real, living wife. Up until then, when I looked into her eyes, I always saw the ghost of the wife I'd never had. But for the first time, I saw my living wife in them. She was telling the truth. She wasn't going to kill herself. We had a deal.

Just a moment later, I let all the water drain back into the lake. And you, daroga—you were in bad shape. I thought for sure you were done for. But there you were, alive. I had promised to take both of you back up to the surface, and I kept my word. Once I got you out of the Louis-Philippe room, I went back alone.

"What did you do with the Vicomte de Chagny?" the Persian interrupted.

Ah, well, you see, I couldn't just carry him out right away. He was my hostage. But I couldn't keep him in the lake house either—not with Christine there. So I locked him up nice and tight. I chained him gently—he was as limp as a rag from the scent of Mazenderan—and left him in the Communists' dungeon, deep below the fifth cellar where no one goes, and no one hears you. Then I came back to Christine. She was waiting for me.

Erik stood up slowly. As he kept talking, his emotions overwhelmed him. He trembled like a leaf.

Yes, she was there. She waited for me—standing, alive, like a real bride. She said she wanted to be saved. And when I stepped forward, more nervous than a little child, she didn't run away. No—she stayed. She waited for me. I even think—yes, I really believe—she tilted her head slightly forward... just a little... like a bride waiting to be kissed.

And then... I kissed her! I did! And she didn't die!

Oh, daroga, it's such a wonderful thing—to kiss someone on the forehead. You can't imagine it! But I—I can! My own mother, daroga, my poor, unhappy mother—she never let me kiss her. She would run away and toss me my mask instead. And no other woman ever let me kiss her either. Never, not once! You can't understand how happy I was. I cried. I fell at her feet and cried. And I kissed her feet—her tiny feet—still crying.

You're crying too, daroga. She cried as well. That angel cried...

Erik's sobs grew louder, and even the Persian couldn't hold back his tears while watching the masked man, his shoulders shaking, clutching at his chest—torn between love and sorrow.

Yes, daroga... I felt her tears on my forehead... they were soft... they were sweet. They slipped under my mask and mixed with my own tears. They ran down to my lips...

Listen, daroga—listen to what I did. I took off my mask so I wouldn't miss a single tear. And she didn't run away! She didn't die! She stayed with me... crying with me. We cried together.

That was the greatest happiness I've ever known.

Erik sank into a chair, struggling to breathe.

Ah... I'm not going to die just yet... soon, but not yet... let me cry first.

Listen, daroga... one more thing. While I was at her feet, I heard her whisper, "Poor, unhappy Erik..." and then she took my hand! I had become nothing more than a poor, loyal dog, willing to die for her. I mean it.

In my hand, I held a gold ring—the one I had given her before. She had lost it, and I had found it again. A wedding ring, you see. I slipped it into her hand and said, "Take it... take it for you and him. Let it be my wedding gift—a gift from poor, unhappy Erik. I know you love him... so don't cry anymore."

She asked me gently what I meant. And I made her understand: I was only a sad, faithful dog, ready to die for her. But now she could marry the young man whenever she wanted—because she had cried with me... and shared her tears with mine.

Erik was so emotional that he told the Persian not to look at him— he was choking up and needed to take off his mask. The Persian quietly walked over to the window and opened it. His heart was filled with sympathy, but he kept his eyes on the trees in the Tuileries garden, not wanting to see Erik's bare face.

"I went and freed the young man," Erik said. "Then I brought him to Christine... They kissed in front of me, right there in the Louis-Philippe room. Christine was wearing the ring I gave her. I made her promise that, after I was dead, she would come back one night— crossing the lake from the Rue Scribe side—and secretly bury me with the ring. I told her exactly where to find my body and what to do with it... Then Christine kissed me, for the first time, right here—on my forehead. Don't look, daroga! Right here, on my forehead—mine! Don't look... And then they left, the two of them. Christine had stopped crying... I was the only one who cried... Daroga, daroga, if she keeps her promise, she'll come back soon!"

The Persian didn't ask any more questions. He felt sure that Raoul and Christine were safe. No one could listen to Erik's voice that night—full of tears—and doubt what he said.

Erik put his mask back on and gathered his strength to leave. He told the Persian that, when he felt death coming, he would send him the thing he valued most in the world: Christine's letters, which she had written for Raoul and left with Erik, along with a few of her belongings—some gloves, a shoe buckle, and two handkerchiefs. When the Persian asked more, Erik explained that, as soon as Raoul and Christine were free, they had planned to find a priest and quietly get married somewhere far away where no one could find them. He said they had taken a train from "the northern railway station of the world."

Finally, Erik asked the Persian to tell the young couple about his death once he received the promised letters and keepsakes. He also asked him to put a small notice in the newspaper Epoque to let the world know he had passed.

That was it. The Persian walked Erik to the door, and Darius helped him down to the street. A cab was waiting. Erik climbed in, and the Persian, watching from the window, heard him tell the driver:

"Take me to the Opera."

The cab drove off into the night.

That was the last time the Persian ever saw poor, lonely Erik.

Three weeks later, the Epoque printed a simple notice:

"Erik is dead."

Epilogue

I've now shared the strange but true story of the Opera Ghost. As I said at the start, no one can deny that Erik really existed. Today, there's plenty of evidence to prove that he lived, and we can trace his actions clearly through everything that happened to the Chagny family.

There's no need to repeat how much this case shocked Paris. The kidnapping of the singer, the strange death of Count Philippe de Chagny, the disappearance of his brother Raoul, and the drugging of the gasman and his assistants at the Opera—so many tragedies, so much drama and mystery surrounded the love story of Raoul and the sweet Christine. What happened to that amazing, mysterious artist, the one the world would never hear from again? Most people thought she was caught between two jealous brothers. No one guessed the truth. No one realized that both Christine and Raoul had quietly left the world behind to live happily ever after in secret—especially after Count Philippe's unexplained death. One day, they simply boarded a train at "the northern railway station of the world."

Maybe someday I'll take that same train, and in the quiet lands of Norway or somewhere in Scandinavia, I'll search near the lakes for signs of Raoul and Christine—or even Mamma Valerius, who disappeared at the same time. Maybe, just maybe, I'll hear the faraway echo of her voice, the voice of the girl who once knew the Angel of Music.

Even long after the case had been officially filed away by the unimaginative Judge Faure, some newspapers tried from time to time to uncover the truth. Only one paper, which specialized in theater gossip, dared to write:

"We recognize the work of the Opera Ghost."

Even that was meant as a joke.

Only the Persian knew the full truth, along with the strongest proof—those final relics Erik had promised him. I was lucky enough to help complete that proof, with the daroga's guidance. I kept him updated every day on what I discovered, and he helped steer my search. He hadn't set foot in the Opera in many years, but he still remembered every detail of the building and helped me find its most hidden passages. He told me where to look next and who to talk to. He even sent me to visit Monsieur Poligny, just before the poor man passed away.

I didn't know he was so close to death. I'll never forget how shocked he looked when I asked him about the ghost. He stared at me like I was the devil and only managed a few scattered words—but that was enough. It showed just how disturbed he'd been by O.G. back in the day. Poligny had always been a man of pleasure and excitement, and Erik had clearly rattled him deeply.

When I told the Persian how little I had learned from Poligny, he gave a faint smile and said,

"Poligny never realized how completely Erik fooled him."

The Persian sometimes spoke of Erik like a genius, and sometimes like a criminal. He went on:

"Poligny was superstitious, and Erik knew it. Erik knew almost everything about what went on behind the scenes at the Opera. When Poligny heard a strange voice in Box Five, reminding him how he spent his time and how he'd betrayed his partner's trust, he panicked. At first, he thought it was a voice from heaven and that he was doomed. But when the voice asked him for money, he realized he was being blackmailed. Debienne had been fooled too. Both of them were tired of the job anyway, so they left without digging any deeper into who O.G. really was. They handed the whole mystery over to the new managers and were just glad to be rid of it. To them, the Opera Ghost was just a headache—not an adventure."

I brought up the two new Opera managers and said I was surprised that, in his Memoirs of a Manager, Moncharmin talked a lot about the Opera Ghost at first, but barely mentioned him later. The Persian, who knew the Memoirs like he'd written them himself, told me the answer was in a short passage near the end of the book. Here's what Moncharmin wrote, which is important because it explains how the famous "twenty-thousand francs" incident ended so simply:

As for O.G., who played a few strange tricks that I talked about earlier, I'll just say this: he made up for all the trouble he caused with one unexpected, generous act. I think he realized he had taken the joke too far—especially after we contacted the police. We had even scheduled a meeting with Inspector Mifroid to tell him everything. But just a few days after Christine Daaé went missing, we found a large envelope on Richard's desk. Written on it in red ink were the words: "WITH O.G.'S COMPLIMENTS." Inside was all the money he had temporarily taken from our safe. Richard said we should just let the whole thing go, and I agreed. Everything worked out in the end. What do you say, O.G.?

After the money was returned, Moncharmin believed Richard had been behind the whole ghost story as a prank. Meanwhile, Richard believed Moncharmin made it all up to get back at him for some earlier jokes. Neither of them ever figured out what really happened.

I asked the Persian how the ghost had managed to take the money from Richard's coat pocket, even though it was pinned shut. He said he hadn't looked into that specific trick, but if I wanted to solve it myself, I should check the managers' office. After all, Erik wasn't called the "trap-door lover" for nothing.

I promised to investigate—and when I did, I found exactly what he meant. The evidence was clear and left no doubt that Erik had pulled off everything he was credited with.

With the Persian's story, Christine's notes, the memories of people who had worked under Moncharmin and Richard, and even little Meg Giry—(though her mother, Madame Giry, had sadly passed away)—I put together all the facts. Sorelli, now retired in Louveciennes, also helped. I plan to send everything I've gathered to the archives of the Opera.

I didn't find Erik's hidden house by the lake—he had sealed all the secret entrances. But I did find the hidden passage known as the Communists' road. Its wooden floor was falling apart in places. I also found the trapdoor that Raoul and the Persian had used to enter the cellars. Inside the old prison cell, I saw initials carved into the wall by prisoners. Among them were "R" and "C"—for Raoul de Chagny. The marks are still there today.

If any reader visits the Opera, I suggest they ask for permission to explore freely. Go to Box Five and knock on the large column next to the stage box. It sounds hollow. That's because it is. It's big enough inside for two people. Don't be surprised the ghost's voice came from there. The column looked like solid marble, and the sound always seemed to come from somewhere else—because Erik was a master ventriloquist.

The column is decorated with carvings, and I still hope to discover the exact decoration that opened or closed to allow Erik to send messages to Madame Giry or deliver his gifts.

But none of this compares to my most exciting discovery—made right in the managers' office. Near the desk chair, I found a small trapdoor, about the size of a man's forearm. It opens like the lid of a box. Through it, you could reach up and slip a hand into someone's coat pocket. That's how the money was stolen—and how it was returned.

When I told the Persian about this, I asked if that meant Erik was just having fun with his notebook full of demands. He replied:

Don't believe that for a moment. Erik needed money. He saw himself as different from everyone else and didn't feel like the usual rules applied to him. Because of how badly he was treated for his looks, he used his talents—his quick hands and brilliant mind—to get by. He only returned the money because he didn't need it anymore. He had given up his dream of marrying Christine Daaé. He had let go of everything in the world above.

Erik was born in a small town near Rouen. His father was a skilled builder. As a child, Erik ran away from home because his parents were terrified by how he looked. He spent some time at traveling fairs, where he was displayed as the "living corpse." He traveled all across Europe, performing in fairs and learning magic and music from the Romani people. He became known for his voice, his ventriloquism, and his unbelievable magic tricks.

Eventually, his fame reached the royal palace in Mazenderan, where the Shah's favorite, a bored young princess, heard of him. A fur trader returning from Russia told the court about Erik's performances, and the Persian official known as the daroga was sent to find him. Erik was brought to Persia and became powerful for a time, though he committed some terrible acts. He helped plan assassinations and used his inventions against Persia's enemies. The Shah was impressed.

During this period—what the daroga called "the rosy hours of Mazenderan"—Erik designed a palace full of secret passages and trapdoors, where the Shah could disappear without anyone knowing how. But once the Shah had the palace, he wanted to get rid of Erik so no one else could learn the secrets. He planned to have Erik blinded or killed, along with everyone who had helped build the palace. The daroga, who had grown fond of Erik, helped him escape, risking his own life.

Luckily for the daroga, a body was found near the Caspian Sea dressed in Erik's clothes, and everyone believed it was him. The daroga lost his wealth and was banished, but he was allowed a small monthly pension and later moved to Paris.

Meanwhile, Erik went to Turkey and worked for the Sultan, building the same kinds of hidden doors and rooms he had in Persia. He even created life-sized puppets that looked exactly like the Sultan. These tricks kept people guessing where the real ruler was. But once again, Erik knew too much and had to flee.

He tried to live a normal life, working as a builder of ordinary homes. Eventually, he got a job working on the foundations of the Paris Opera House. Once he discovered the huge cellars underneath, his imagination took over. He was still deeply ashamed of his appearance and decided to create a secret home underground, hidden from the world forever.

The rest of the story is known to you now. Erik wanted to live like a normal person. But he was too hideous, so he had to use his gifts for tricks and shadows instead of fame and respect. If he had looked ordinary, he could have become one of the most brilliant people in the world. His heart was big enough to lead an empire. Instead, he lived and died in a basement.

I prayed over his remains, hoping God would forgive him despite the terrible things he had done. I'm sure I saw his body recently when it was uncovered in the same spot where he once carried Christine Daaé, unconscious, into the depths of the Opera House. I knew it was Erik not by his skull, since death makes all faces look the same, but because he was still wearing the simple gold ring Christine had given him and promised to return with when he died.

Now, what will become of Erik's skeleton? Surely it doesn't belong in an ordinary grave. No—his remains should be kept in the archives of the Paris Opera. This was no ordinary man.

[1] Even so, I am convinced that it would be easy to reach it by draining the lake, as I have repeatedly requested the Ministry of Fine Arts to do. I was speaking about it to M. Dujardin-Beaumetz, the under-secretary for fine arts, only forty-eight hours before the publication of this book. Who knows but that the score of DON JUAN TRIUMPHANT might yet be discovered in the house on the lake?

[2] See the interview of the special correspondent of the MATIN, with Mohammed-Ali Bey, on the day after the entry of the Salonika troops into Constantinople.

THE END

Thank You for Reading

Dear Reader,

We hope this timeless classic has sparked your imagination and enriched your literary journey. Now that you've turned the final page, we want to share a vision for the future of reading—one where every classic you've ever wanted to explore is at your fingertips, in a format that best suits your life.

We'd like to invite you to gain immediate, unlimited digital & audiobook access to hundreds of the most treasured literary classics ever written—along with the option to secure deluxe paperback, hardcover & box set editions at printing cost. Together, we can spark a new global literary renaissance alongside our small, independent publishing house called "The Library of Alexandria."

Thousands of years ago, the Library of Alexandria stood as a beacon of knowledge—until it was lost to history. We aim to reignite that spirit of preservation and discovery right now, in the modern age—only this time, it's accessible to all, in every language and every format.

Picture a world where every timeless classic, novel, poem, or philosophical treatise is not only available to read but also updated for today's readers—modernized, translated into any language or dialect, and ready to enjoy in any format you choose, whether that is in an eBook, audiobook, paperback, or deluxe hardcover & box set version a printing cost.

By joining our movement to rebuild the modern Library of Alexandria, you become part of an unprecedented mission to offer:

- **Unlimited Audiobook & eBook Access to the Greatest Classics of All Time**

  Instantly explore thousands of legendary works, from Plato and Shakespeare to Jane Austen and Leo Tolstoy. All are instantly ready to read or listen to, giving you a complete literary universe at your fingertips.

- **Paperback & Deluxe Editions at Printing Costs:**

  Purchase any title in a paperback, deluxe hardbound, or deluxe boxset edition at printing costs, shipped right to your doorstep. Curate your personal library of Alexandria with editions worthy of display—crafted to last, designed to captivate, and delivered straight to your door.

- **Modern translations for Contemporary Readers in all languages and dialects**

  Discover a vast selection of classics reimagined in clear, current language—no more struggling with outdated phrases or obscure references. Next to the original versions, we aim to offer translations in as many languages and dialects as possible.

  As we continue our translation efforts and add new languages, readers everywhere can connect with these works as if they were written today. By bridging linguistic divides, you're contributing to ensuring that these timeless stories become more meaningful, accessible, and inspiring for people across the globe.

- **Your Personal Library of Alexandria:**

  Over the months and years, you'll curate a unique physical archive of classics—each volume a testament to your taste, curiosity, and love of knowledge. It's not just about owning books—it's about curating a cultural legacy you'll cherish and pass down for generations to come.

- **Join a Global Literary Renaissance:**

  Your support fuels an ongoing mission: allowing us to reinvest in offering deluxe print editions (including special boxsets) at their true cost, broaden the range of available formats and translations, and extend the reach of these works to new audiences worldwide. By joining today, you're not just preserving a legacy of masterpieces; you set in motion a powerful wave of literary accessibility.

  We are more than a publisher—we're a movement, and we can't do it alone. Your support lets us scale our mission, preserving and reimagining history's greatest works for tomorrow's readers.

Become a Torchbearer of knowledge.

Thank you for picking up this book and allowing us into your literary journey. As you turn the pages, know that you're part of something larger: a global effort to keep these stories alive, share their wisdom across borders and generations, and spark a true cultural revival for the modern era.

If this resonates with you—please consider taking the next step by visiting:

www.libraryofalexandria.com

With gratitude and a shared love of knowledge,

The Modern Library of Alexandria Team

Visit:

www.libraryofalexandria.com

Or scan the code below:

www.ingramcontent.com/pod-product-compliance
Lightning Source LLC
Chambersburg PA
CBHW011351010726
47494CB00008B/2268